The Constitution

Tomorrow's World Order

David Gomadza

First Global President of the World

www.twofuture.world

info@twofuture.world

DEDICATION

"No woman or child shall die needlessly because of wars on our watch. The death of a woman or child is an attack on all of us."

David Gomadza

First Global President of the World

Tomorrow's World Order

\

The Constitution: Tomorrow's World Order.

Table of Contents

xi

ACKNOWLEDGMENTS

Tomorrow's World Order.

OUR PITCH AND THE REQUEST FOR FUNDING.

TOMORROW'S WORLD ORDER

6 EASBY ROAD BRADFORD BD7 1QX UNITED KINGDOM.

REGISTERED IN GREAT BRITAIN REG 2331788

00447719210295

www.twofuture.world

info@twofuture.world

Write a cheque or donate through PayPal or our bank.

2020-2025 Political Fundraising Campaign.

Dear Reader/Donor

Please Take Time To Read As The Issues Raised Are Critical That You Must Fully Understand What Is Happening And What We Stand For. Thank You.

The Problem.

Do you know that the current system is designed to take away money from you through high taxes, and high prices to limit circulating disposable income as a way of controlling inflation. Leaving you poor and future generations poor too? Even if it is not a directly intended aim by the government but that is how the system works. This is because the only new source of money is through printing. FACT. To make things worse the system creates so many social issues. In order to trigger it to come for the second time and take even more money from you through donations and charity contributions. This is not a coincidence but a preplanned but unfair barbaric system that benefits only the government as they let you fight and do what they are supposed to solve. Exempting themselves from their duty, saving money and making all of you even poorer. Taking advantage of your generosity and kindness. So, what is the use of paying taxes etc.? Surely with the donations and money raised so far things should have improved but now they are even creating digital weapons, watermarks, and digital pathogens to steal even more money from you. Leaving you all empty as they use your fears to steal from you as you contribute towards eliminating these. FACT!

The current system is designed in such a way that it exonerates the police or doctors for wrongfully killing or abusing you through e.g., shootings, harassment, and torture because you pay them through taxes for whatever they do to you. Their salaries are paid by your contributions. The judges will simply clear them because you bought whatever they are selling, meaning all things they do to you. As you are funding them. Self-inflicted wounds have no grounds to complain. Only you are to blame. Are you surprised they all get acquitted in all murder cases etc.?

The current system is gangster minded. Barbaric and meant for uncivilized societies and times. In that it centers around weapons manufacturing and using the weapons to get all the resources they can't' afford. No matter how harsh that sounds. This is the truth, would you be surprised to see the large number of wars, sanctions, invasions, assassinations etc., all financial crisis, high unemployment, high taxes, human rights violations, social unrest, stupid killings by the police and the hospitals of innocent.

civilians, civil unrest, taking us back to the 1980s, torture, human hacking, poor living standards for the past seventy-five years, stagnating economies, poor old infrastructure, poor old transport systems, and poor government practices and all climatic issues. For with the little resources, they have. They make guns and use the guns to get everything they need and can't afford at Gunpoint.

Your critical role. Our solutions are for everyone, including future generations. So be part of this. Get in.

Do you know the current system was put in place just after the Second World War? And the people behind this are either dead or old. No wonder we have all the above problems. Simply because things then were not the same as now. The system was not meant for us, the Future Generations. To make things worse they lacked foresight to anticipate what we need and what future generations want.

The Solutions.

So, a system change is our critical goal. We need a system that reflects today's thinking and addresses today's problems, not a seventy-five-year-old OBSOLETE system.

Your Great Financial Contribution.

But to do this requires great financial commitment. So, we need your help. Get involved and be part of this. This is not just for us

TWO alone. No, but for all humanity. Do this either for yourselves, your kids or just for future generations. You can help greatly because your support is the KEY to solving all global problems we have today.

There is a great misconception that there are other solutions to all global problems because if that was true, they could have solved all the problems by now. Given the fact that for the past 75 years our fathers and mothers have been asked to donate and make a difference, I tell you this. That the problems then are still the problems now. Even worse now. The current system is designed to rip you off even the few monies you have. This is through high taxes, donations, high prices, and your charity contributions as a way of removing money in the system to fight inflation without solving the real problems. Thereby creating a vicious circle. FACT.

But we are here to solve the problems. A sure solution. Put a new system for us and future generations.

Make the government Accountable and stop neglecting their duties knowing that you will contribute toward eliminating the problems they created or neglected in the first place. They must be held to account. We will see to that.

A new system of global, national, and individual planning.

Stop anything that takes money from you. Paying taxes, making donations to the government institutions because they created and failed to solve problems. So that you take over and then take money away from you. For example, we will stop money to be left to the government when someone dies.

But we will create an extra individual savings account that we use as collateral to fund you and pay for services like medical insurance, loans, mortgages etc. We will still deduct money from your salaries and wages but this money goes to your savings account. Which you will have access to at a certain age or if the balance reaches a certain amount.

We will stop wars, weapons manufacturing, stocking, and distribution, we will stop sanctions globally. We will stop all evil acts going on right now, mainly the needlessly killings of women and children.

We will invest in brand new cities for us and the future generations. These must be energy efficient and must use safe renewable materials etc. This enables us indirectly to fight climate change as we will also put emphasis on renewable sources of energy etc. with the aim to ban reliance on fossil fuels alone, in the future.

We will bring law and order through our court system and the right enforcement and policing. Our people will never kill innocent civilians simply because they will be competent enough and know the law can't let them get away with murder.

I am excited about all this as I have a lot to tell you when I have written a book about all this, titled Tomorrow's World Order. But I know your time is special so in short, to introduce a new system your donations will help us put this new system in place. We will have our own money printing rights and our own digital currency, so your contributions are to only propulsive launch us. Meaning they are short term and not perpetual like with the current system. So, your donations are going to empower and improve the living conditions of everyone. Do you know that some great nations are here today from the simple realization that the system was corrupt and unfair to them? Making them refuse paying taxes to be used to exempt the government from their duty of solving the issues themselves? Just think about that!

I can't stress enough how important your donations are to us and how critical they are to the successful launch of our party and the new system which we will put in place. So, Donate Today generously so that you will never donate or lose money in the future exempting those responsible for such issues. This is because our system will eliminate all the problems, they use to steal money from you forever. FACT!

Call to action.

It's critical that you donate today. It has been an urgent matter for decades only that few knew how corrupt and unfair the system is or that the few who knew about this had been silenced through assassinations etc. Our solution is for the future as we aim to raise living standards to levels never thought of before. And also, to bring wealth to all humanity at levels you can only dream of right now. Imagine all the money you pay as taxes and donations and all sorts being yours in your savings account? Imagine having a government-held but your second savings account? Imagine never spending a penny on things like charity work, things the government should be tackling? Not for them to indirectly delegate to you when you are paying high taxes etc. to solve just that.

Imagine brand new cities, new buildings, new infrastructure, and clean transport systems?

Imagine a world brought together by the advancement in

technology raising people's self-esteem to levels you can only dream of?

I say take charge of your life and don't trust anyone else to do better things for you. The fact that the government staff; the police and hospitals and doctors etc. are at the forefront of killing innocent people. That in itself is a revelation about a system failure. An incompetent cruel and abusive system that is so obsolete you can't imagine it is still existing.

Choose better things simply because you, Damn Right! Deserve the best. So, join the best as well. Get in! Get involved. Why accept mediocre lives? Why go with the flow? When you can have the best life can offer. If you are a hardliner raised that way, why not do this for your kids and for future generations?

Only Tomorrow's World Order has the answers as we tackle the real problem. The need for a system change. Open your eyes and fight for what is rightfully yours. We can only show you what they sweep under the seats. But the final decision is yours. Don't leave things to chance.

Donate today and let's begin an exciting new journey to a better, more advanced stage of development. Where living standards are so high, and wealth is for everyone as their system keeps taking from you. Our brand-new system will keep giving you. What is not to like? A peaceful world, with rich highly self

esteemed people who all work together for. Surely with the donations and money raised so far things should have improved. But now they are even creating digital weapons, watermarks, and digital pathogens to steal even more money from you.

Never be fooled, there are no other solutions. Just simply stealing money from you to make you all even poorer so they have jobs and reasons to screw all of you up. Pardon my language but that is a fact.

Donate today.

Sincerely

On behalf of.

David Gomadza

The First Global President of The World

Signed. DavidGomadza.

20 October 2020

Updated 23 November 2023

Founder and Political Party Leader

Tomorrow's World Order

www.twofuture.world

info@twofuture.world

00447719210295

THE CONSTITUTION

Tomorrow's World Order Founder and President

David Gomadza

Updated 03 March 2020 & 23 November 2023

For consistency as in the constitution and the financial scheme.

The party leader is David Gomadza

Treasurer is David Gomadza

Nominating Officer is David Gomadza

Campaign Officer is Bogdan Gavrila.

WELCOME

You have taken a great step by choosing to read this constitution.

Reading alone is one step of the process. You must join us too. We promise to change the world as you know it today. We promise to bring wealth to all mankind to levels never experienced before. We are going to introduce a new system from national to global governance, financial planning, and management. We are going to introduce a new system that will revolutionize the world you know today. We are going to increase the wealth of individuals, nations and globally to levels never thought of before. We have the answers to all global problems. We have a solution to global debt, poverty, financial crisis, unemployment, stagnant development for the past seventy years and above all; all human rights abuses. Yes, we have a solution for everything. We adopted a holistic approach and as such our party must be in power throughout the globe so that we can synchronize the implementation of the new global system of governance, fiscal management, and the judiciary system. Yes, you must choose us and vote for our candidates. We believe mankind has been stuck in defensive stages in which mankind has affordability issues and instead with the little resources he has; makes weapons which he goes on to use through force, wars, invasions, sanctions, intimidation, and all evil acts to get the expensive resources he can't afford like oil. To make things worse, in the process kill innocent women and children. Yes, mankind has relied on weapons and the defense as a driver of the

economy. But we are saying we as Tomorrow's World Order and I as the Founder and President there is a solution. Yes, an answer to all this. I believe the current system is now obsolete and only a new system is a must hence the rise of Tomorrow's World Order and our new perfect system will bring wealth to all mankind to levels never witnessed before.

Ladies and gentlemen, boys and girls JOIN US TODAY for a new chapter in mankind's development journey. Signed

David Gomadza

Founder and President

Tomorrow's World Order.

07 August 2019

Updated

03 March 2020

&

23 November 2023

OUR PARTY LABELS

Establishing our legal name and enabling our party to be easily identified. THE CONSTITUTION These are Tomorrow's World Order's written rules and laws that we use to structure and manage the affairs of the political party.

TOMORROW'S WORLD ORDER

2. ARTICLE 1

3. NAME OF THE PARTY

1. The name of this political party shall be [Tomorrow's World Order] United Kingdom hereinafter referred to as the party. The party can be abbreviated as T.W.O [UK].

2. Our logo is a hand in a victory or T.W.O sign with the inside of the hand facing forward. T.W.O[UK] is a constituent country-specific part of

Tomorrow's World Order [Global] and is subject to its rules and

constitution.

3. Our slogan is Your Future, Your Say.

4. The geographic area of T.W.O [UK] is in all England, Scotland, and Wales.

PREAMBLE

1. We ask [Tomorrow's World Order].

2. We intend to register on the Great Britain register with the intention to contest elections in all England, Scotland, and Wales (Great Britain

register).

3. [Tomorrow's World Order] party intends to contest elections in UK's parliamentary general elections in all of England, Scotland, and Wales.

4. Through our constitution and the adopted Financial Scheme of

[Tomorrow's World Order], the party has processes in place to comply with the rules that govern the election and financial activities of our party. 5. See our constitution and the attached Financial Scheme in Article 20 that our party has adopted. In all our dealings within the United Kingdom and globally we confirm that our constitution and how Tomorrow's World Order as a party operates, adhere to all principles of full equality, and comply with the Equality and Human Rights Commission rules, laws and

regulations.

6. For clarity, any reference to masculine in this constitution can be a reference to any; either feminine or masculine.

7. We shall adopt an Affirmative Action policy: that makes us comply with gender and equality laws as such we shall adopt a 40:40:20 % rule.

8. This means we shall aim to have an equal number of women and men in most of our organizations, committees, and branches.

9. That means forty percent shall be women and forty percent men with twenty percent made up of either gender. We as Tomorrow World Order [UK] declare that as a political party to be established in the United Kingdom, we shall observe the rules and regulations

in our conduct as a political party as stated in the Political Party, Election and Referendum Act 2000.

10. Our party T.W.O [UK] shall act fair and not favor people due to their religious beliefs, sex, race, education, other beliefs, ethnic origin, class,

sexual orientation, etc. the list is not exhaustive.

11. We as T.W.O [UK] in conducting all our activities shall observe the requirements placed upon us by the United Kingdom of observing the rule of law, democracy, liberty, and all human rights.

5. ARTICLE 2

6. PURPOSE AND OUR UNIQUE POLITICAL PHILOSOPHY

7. ORIGINS.

1. Tomorrow's World Order arose out of the realization that mankind for the past 2000 years has been stuck in defensive stages of development where he can't afford to buy everything he needs and instead with the little he has designs and makes weapons which he then uses to get everything else he needs by force, through wars, invasions, assassinations, sanctions and all kinds of evil; in the process killing innocent women and children; people who are the voiceless and defenseless of any society.

2. Yet there is a system that will increase individual, national, and global wealth to levels never imagined before. A system that makes everyone afford to buy any resources at market value. Yes, a new system of governance and fiscal planning and management that will revolutionize global wealth and

development.

3. The major factor is the fact that a new system is a must and urgently needed. 4. The current system is obsolete and not-fit-for purpose, yet we still use it despite several financial crises with the 2008 being the last major one, global poverty, global debt above $244 trillion, mediocre living standards for the past seventy years and stagnating economies with some developed nations falling back into developing nations. Poor fiscal planning and management everywhere when there is an answer. I aim to introduce a new system of governance and financial planning that will eliminate global, country, and individual debt. Increase wealth, raise living standards, and make everyone witness wealth never dreamt of globally at the same time installing the rule of law.

2

8. ARTICLE 3

9. FUNCTIONS AND OBJECTIVES OF PARTY

1. The first aim and the objective of Tomorrow's World Order is to endorse our selected candidates to contest, win and take roles as the Prime Minister or President or

Chancellor, etc. through the General, Parliamentary and or the Presidential

elections and to participate in all elections; to be selected for roles in the House of Commons, the Senate and the House of Representations depending on the country in question.

10. THE AIM OF T.W.O [UK]

2. Is to represent Tomorrow's World Order [Global] in the United Kingdom that is in England, Scotland and Wales promoting its views and principles as in its constitution.

11. THE PURPOSE OF THIS PARTY SHALL BE.
3. To contest elections and win positions and seats in all elections and at all levels of the government and one day to win the leadership contest so that our political party will be the ruling party in the United Kingdom that is in England, Scotland, and Wales.

4. To write, develop, publicize, and promote the views of Tomorrow's World Order [Global] in the United Kingdom that is in all England, Scotland and Wales and applying these on a national scale with the aim of taking

humanity to another level of development, bringing in wealth to all humankind at levels never seen before through our policies, procedures, and rules.

5. We as a people have the potential to achieve great yet we are operating below our optimal levels.

6. We aim to change mankind's thinking of emphasizing austerity measures and show all humankind that growth is the only answer to all global and

national problems: the way nature intended.

7. Prosperity to all humankind and not just to the few privileged ones.

8. To plan, organize, promote, and take part in all peaceful activities within the United Kingdom.

9. To advance our agendas and gain the trust, support, and backing of all the people and convince all that only our policies are the only real solutions; the only way forward.

10. We have heard and seen all current policies in play, and we already know the disappointing outcome and now it's time for change and change can only mean growth and levels of wealth for

all never experienced before. We have the answers.

11. We aim to participate in all elections and referendums at all levels,

12. We aim to take all won seats and where there is ambiguity the party leader must decide. If doubt still exists, the national party leader can put the matter before the global leader of Tomorrow's World Order unless it is the same person in which case he has, or she has to decide therein.

13. The elected members represent our party at all levels and advance our goals and objectives.

14. The national party for that region here T.W.O [UK] will link and cooperate with the main party T.W.O [Global] and with other local institutions,

bodies or even other charities, etc. for the sake of carrying out their duties as in the constitution or where the leader sees fit.

12. OBJECTIVES OF TOMORROW'S WORLD ORDER AT NATIONAL AND GLOBAL SCALE.

1. To introduce a new system of governance both at a national and global scale that emphasizes the printing of new money as the only true source of growth and individual, national, and global wealth.

2. To shift the thinking from austerity: living within your means, to an emphasis on growth giving the people more power in decisions and policies that affect them.

3. To bring to all humankind wealth levels never experienced before.

4. To protect already accumulated wealth and put things in place to make sure that this wealth is passed on from generation to generation rather than be taken by the government or institutions or

charities.

5. To protect savings already accumulated and put things in place so that these savings often accumulated over the years will not be lost in a short period of time.

6. To introduce a health plan that is free but fair where all citizens have to maintain a balance in their government-owned-yet-individual savings account above a certain level to qualify for free health, with the government using this savings account as collateral to offer free services. The government, depending on circumstances, can match the balance, double it, triple it, or even multiply this tenfold in order to provide enough cover.

7. To abolish the taking of wealth of the deceased-without-relatives by the government.

8. To ban donations of wealth especially by the elderly to government,

institutions like hospitals and or charities. Wealth to be left to relatives only and even distant relatives rather than the government, institutions like

hospitals and charities.

9. To abolish income tax payments and collection by the government.

10. To ban payments of national insurance and collection of these by the government.

11. To introduce instead a collection from the income of a single-digit-figure initially and opening of an individual savings-but government-owned

account. An account that will be held by the government until a time when a person reaches a certain age, or the savings account balance reaches a certain amount before the person has access to it.

12. To introduce a new government-backing of its citizens policy where it is indebted to its people; where it bails-out the people instead of banks first, a system where governments are mandated to protect the wealth of its citizens and are proactive to cushion the wealth by providing loans, mortgages, etc. through the individual savings-yet-government held account.

13. Instead of collecting taxes and national insurance from income and wages the government shall collect savings straight to the citizen's savings account which the government will use to assess eligibility levels for free health, loans, mortgages and pension support, the account remains in possession of the

government until such a time when the individual reaches a certain age, say 60 to have access to it and or if the contribution balance reaches a certain value e.g., $100 000 for argument's sake then the person can have access to it.

14. This individual savings-yet government-held account's balance will act as collateral in order for the government to offer free health, loans, mortgages, etc.

15. To advance and promote the printing of new money as the only true source of growth and wealth to a level never seen before with 5-year cycles of printing. 16. To introduce a new system to deal with hyperinflation and all issues associated with the printing of new money.

17. To introduce a new system where all nations on earth must adopt our digital currency as the New Single Reserve Global Currency [NSRGC] to take humanity to levels never seen before.

18. To advance a system where all nations on earth will use two

currencies as the base currencies namely their own sovereign national currency as the first currency and secondly adopt and use our digital currency

FutureGoldCoin as the second base currency, even though nations can use more than two currencies these must be the two critical currencies to achieve growth and wealth to levels never experienced before.

19. To advance and lay a new system and framework of global governance where there is the rule of law, democracy, peace, and wealth for all to new heights. A system adhered to by all simply because the system represents everyone and is for all, an effective system.

20. To introduce a new system of analyzing debt and dealing with individual, national, and global debt and a new system of treating debt as having a depreciation value.

21. To introduce a new system that encourages individual, national and global savings, introducing the government-owned yet individual savings accounts, introducing Tomorrow's World Order Global Reserve Bank where all nations after printing new money have to deposit this new money in the Global Reserve Bank as savings which we will treat as collateral and offer them the equivalent of our universal global digital currency the FutureGoldCoin which they must use in their economy to achieve growth to new heights.

22. To introduce a new system that will take humanity to the next stage of development away from the defensive stage in which we are stuck in; where humankind makes weapons cheaper and then uses the weapons to get the expensive resources like oil.

23. To introduce a new system that will increase affordability to levels high enough to buy any resources be it oil etc. at market

prices instead of relying on weapons to fetch these.

24. To introduce new laws and regulations to offer peace and consolation to those who seek justice and on the other hand, introduce a new universal justice system that is fair and effective and feared by all, regardless.

25. To maintain individual differences in people and nations brought by mother nature recognizing this as everyone's right by not insisting or imposing changes but maintaining individualism as long as the differences are within the law. That means preserving the nation-specific difference, strengthening the borders of each nation as desired as long as all are willing to abide by all international laws and our rules and regulations. Encouraging diversity.

26. Bringing peace to all humankind with the aim of networking and cooperating together on a global scale.

27. To introduce a global leader who is not biased; a leader that represents all mankind and one who is for the people globally, one to lead all nations acting as an overseer and the guiding force with the aim of taking humanity out of the defensive stages where weapons and defense take center stage.

13. ACHIEVING THE ABOVE GOALS AND OBJECTIVES WILL ENABLE US TO BE ABLE TO.
1. Provide employment to all and make working worth it as income tax and national insurance will have been abolished. An extra savings accounts for everyone.

2. Will enable us to achieve income equality and distribute income fairly.

3. Make us able to build brand new cities from scratch and provide excellent infrastructure that meets today's standards.

4. Increase living standards.

5. Protect the wealth and savings of everyone, cushioning people against all kinds of crisis, therefore, improving living conditions and standards.

14. GLOBALLY OUR OBJECTIVES ARE.

1. To ban global wars, weapons manufacturing, possession, and trading. 2. To ban the killings of innocent women and children globally.

3. To ban all kinds of sanctions [which arose out of the 'Scorched Earth' policies of the 1900] that affect the voiceless; women and children.

4. This will enable us to introduce and put into place a system that guarantees human rights for all and freedoms in the process of improving the quality of life and living standards.

5. To achieve all this, we aim to appoint people who we will field-in all democratic elections at all levels with the aim to win seats and office so that in the end our appointed and elected leaders become the rulers and leaders of the United Kingdom in all England, Scotland, and Wales and globally.

Leaders from Tomorrow's World Order must increase wealth levels to levels never

experienced before, empower all and bring peace to all while improving life, quality of life and raising everyone's self-esteem to levels never thought of; the only way nature intended. Only Tomorrow's World Order has the

answers.

RIGHTS TO PRINT OUR OWN FIAT MONEY.
When fully operational we shall have the right to print and own our

own paper / fiat money. We shall have powers to design, print and manage our own fiat money called Global Transaction Payment Solution [GTPS]. We shall have digital currency as well as fiat money. Ther quantities of which shall be decided by the political party leader of Tomorrow's World Order [David Gomadza].

15. RIGHTS OF THE CITIZENS

1. We as Tomorrow's World Order strongly believe that affordability or it lack is the root of all problems regarding human rights abuses. Tackling the lack of affordability is the answer to a globe that upholds the rule of law.

2. So, even though human rights play a critical role to us; our emphasis is on tackling the root cause and then letting our justice system bring law and order. 3. This constitution might not deal a lot with the rights of people etc. We strongly believe that solving affordability will automatically bring the rule of law to all. We believe there is a strong causal-effect relationship nevertheless we shall address these rights here.

4. The law gives everyone equal rights before it.

16. RIGHT TO LIFE

1. Everyone shall have the right to life which means the right not to be killed needlessly. We have introduced new laws dealing with women and children's killers through our laws.

2. We have put new laws to ban wars globally.

3. Now it is illegal to consider women and children as collateral damage. Wars and invasions that kill women and children will get the leaders who ordered these wars or commanded these to be dragged to court.

4. Soldier's lives are now protected by our laws. It is illegal to send soldiers to war when the chances of dying or being maimed are

high.

5. Our system has eliminated the reasons for going to war. Every nation will be able to afford to buy any resources. All nations will have enough money to meet basic needs and cooperate with rebels.

6. Sanctions based on the scorched-earth-principles of starving into submission, therefore, are banned.

7. We ban all sanctions that result in the deaths and suffering of women globally. Sanctions target women and children for the leaders to submit to the demands. We say no to such evil thinking.

8. To deal with violators we have introduced the E-laws. These are the

Empathy Laws.

9. They are not discrimination laws but laws that arise since it is human nature not to relate to things, we are not familiar with.

10. Distant things are not close to us. Most people advocate for things that are close to them that they know and are familiar with.

11. Since Tomorrow's World Order is a global political party, your enemies are protected by our laws that make you answerable to us. You can see now that there are no longer loopholes, the main reason why we now banned wars. Any future wars will result in those involved facing our justice system, in fact.

17. EVERYONE HAS RIGHTS TO THE BEST QUALITY OF LIFE.
1. Governments around the globe have greater responsibilities when it comes to quality of life. Some countries are still practicing eugenics movements.

Secretly loading their people with watermarks to protect them and disfiguring others with viral-digital and bio watermarks to justify.

conserving their own. Some governments are hacking and chipping.

Everyone at birth with radiation-emitting devices as a population control and in the process lowering quality of life to medieval times with people looking like zombies etc. All violations of our laws.

2. All acts that violate the quality of life are banned by our constitution and laws.

3. We banned reliance on fossils and equipment, vehicles and infrastructure using these to be phased out. Pollution lowers quality of life. The

constitution mandates the government to invest in research and

development for cheaper cleaner alternatives.

4. We are to embark on new city development schemes to improve the quality of life.

18. RIGHTS TO DEFEND ONESELF.
1. Every person and country on earth has the right to defend itself. Depending on the threat at hand, some countries and people can and might be justified in the use of force to defend themselves. If the threat is formidable and if not

doing anything can be regarded as unreasonable then the right to self-defend can be called upon and that person can seek international help.

19. GENDER EQUALITY LAWS.
1. All people are equal regardless of gender and our constitution places

requirements for all members to observe equality laws in carrying out all activities. During formation, the procedural rules must be considered, and equal representation be applied in all cases with the correct representation number to be adopted. Women have the same opportunities for the top jobs in the party.

20. GENDER IN CANDIDATE LISTING.

1. A system must be adopted and made into bylaws to ensure a certain number of candidates will be selected because they are women, so we have a

representation that is just. Ideally, 50% must be women but a third is the working minimum guideline depending on the number sort.

21. GENDER IN THE DECISION-MAKING PROCESS.

1. In the decision-making committees and executives more must be done to include more women. Ideally, a large number must be women or 50%

whichever is lower. Wars kill more women and children than men and we give women special privileges to be part of the decision-making process to help make policies that reduce their risks of being the victims of wars,

sanctions, and invasions.

22. ARTICLE 4

23. MEMBERSHIP RIGHTS, ROLES, AND RESPONSIBILITIES

24. MEMBERSHIP REQUIREMENTS

1. This part deals with membership of the party.

2. In short, anyone can join as long as they agree to be governed by this constitution and our values and declare and promise that they

believe and relate to our values and objectives. This part explains the roles of all members and what is expected of them. 3. As a general rule; members can resign in writing.

4. Membership can be revoked due to several factors e.g., disregarding the constitution and other laws and acting in competition with the party etc. details below.

5. Non-payment cannot result in cessation of membership as a Membership Payment Buffer account is to be set up to cover non-payments.

6. But non-payment for a year or more might make that membership be regarded as ended.

25. RULES ON MEMBERSHIP OF [TOMORROW'S WORLD ORDER].
1. Minimum age 16.

2. Putting things in place to ensure compliance with the constitution, bylaws, and other laws. For the sake of membership and employment everyone who

becomes our member, and those employed by us will be considered as

having fully declared their willingness and express agreement in writing to be governed by our constitution and our party rules.

3. Members can be asked to sign a document stating the above at initial registration or when taking up employment with T.W.O [UK].

4. To declare not to do or be involved in acts that contradict what we stand for or what is regarded as breaking the laws of the UK and all nations we

operate in.

5. If it later comes to light that such a person has disregarded our constitution from the date the constitution comes into effect and thereafter and any rules and has been involved in acts that are against any laws of the UK and all other countries we are established such a person will automatically cease to become a member and or employee of T.W.O [UK] and T.W.O [Global] and the party leader of the country concerned or any delegated person will dismiss that individual from the party so as not to tarnish the party as long as the person can attend a meeting with party members before the dismissal for his or her case to be heard, where he can attend with a friend, and a

member of T.W.O be provided to be on his side and any appeals to be.

lodged within four weeks.

6. The general body of T.W.O [UK] shall be composed of all members in the United Kingdom including all England, Scotland, and Wales who have

joined, registered, and paid the joining fee or subscription fee and whose.

accounts are up to date having paid all monthly or annual fees, etc. and all new who intend to register and or are in the process of joining.

7. Membership is open to all regardless of age, sex, race, color, sex, creed, gender identity, sexual orientation, disability, socioeconomic status,

national origin, etc. This list is not exhaustive.

26. A MEMBER HERE IS ANYONE.

1. willing to advance our aims and become part of this great movement, 2. willing to follow and abide by the rules of T.W.O [UK] and its

constitution,

3. willing to pay the joining fee and or the subscription irrespective of their previous political affiliation as long as they declare that on becoming a

member this is the only party they will belong to thereafter.

4. Membership starts when the correct fee has been paid and the person registered in the electronic or physical register.

5. The members will be responsible for paying the annual membership fee to be decided at the first annual general meeting.

6. The membership secretary is responsible for maintaining and keeping the membership list. The party leader or secretary can appoint the membership secretary.

27. AN ACTIVE MEMBER SHOULD NOT BE.

1. Someone who has not paid fees for more than 3 months, [but non-payment cannot lead to cessation of membership the Membership Buffer Fund is to be used to pay-off what that person owes],

2. Someone who is facing disciplinary that can lead to expulsion,

3. Someone who has joined another party that is way different from the values we stand for e.g., a party that is restrictive and or does not obey equality laws, etc.

4. All members have to have a registered email address or other

electronic or physical form e.g., correspondence address in order to receive monthly updates and news about the party and to participate fully in all activities regarding the party T.W.O [UK].

5. All members subscribe to our mailing list by subscribing or sending an email to info@twofuture.world

6. The privileges and responsibilities of membership are.

7. Members on merit can apply to be elected to certain party roles and join committees or put their names forward to be elected to different posts from the moment they join the party.

8. But some jobs might, where necessary, insist that members be enrolled for a certain period and to have paid subscription fees for a certain period before taking certain roles like Party Leader and Secretary.

9. As a rule, 3 months with fully paid fees is enough for a member to be elected to certain posts. Six months with the party before being considered to take certain posts but again this shall be at the discretion of the Party Leader and the National Executive Power.

10. A special membership recruitment team can be temporarily appointed to drive the membership recruitment by recruiting members collecting membership details and banks account for subscriptions with the aim of making permanent members the new recruits. In all cases the code of conduct in this constitution and bylaws are to be observed at all times. We shall have different membership categories with executive members paying more than branch members etc. and any acts of dishonesty in dealing with the recruitment process and

subscription can initiate the disciplinary process so as the withholding of funds for personal use which can be regarded as embezzlement. Everyone follows our code of conduct at every time.

11. To take part in the campaign and attend all meetings and if elected to officers' roles to vote and participate fully in the activities of the organization.

12. To acknowledge that any member will abide by the constitution and our rules and to declare that they have no intention to act as in conflict with the party and what we stand for.

13. To pay monthly subscription fees and where a person has not paid for a year and did not express the promise to pay will be regarded as cease being a member.

14. All members have duties to abide by the constitutions and our rules

15. Any acts in conflict or contrary to what we stand for or competition with other members and the party will lead a member to disciplinary action. 16. Members who have not settled their subscription accounts have no voting rights they are considered for the three months they have not settled as

dormant members and as such have no rights and powers to vote or be.

expected to choose new members but can take part in all other party activities. Unless they made other arrangements or promised to pay at a specific date which must not be more than 30 days ahead.

17. Those abroad can form parties in the specific countries, but members can have dual membership of the same party Tomorrow's World Order and that can stand as long as they pay membership fees in both parties but ideally must cease to be a member of one branch and shall be regarded as transferred to the new branch.

18. If they pay membership to both branches of the UK and Global branch in the UK if they live abroad shall be regarded as belonging to the Global branch but will have voting rights in the UK if they return even for a short period.

19. An active member should not be.

20. Members are entitled to 1000 of our digital currency FutureGoldCoin [FCI] depending on availability which will be deposited in their personal digital accounts upon submitting their personal digital wallet address account and paying the membership registration fee. [Subject to change without notice upon the request of the leader]

21. All new members on joining must send their digital wallet address to info@twofuture.world

28. REVOCATION OF MEMBERSHIP.
1. Members can resign on their own but in writing to the membership secretary giving two weeks' notice.

2. Membership may be revoked by Party leadership or any appointed party members delegated to do so due to.

3. acting in conflict with the party rules and constitution,

4. having breached our rules and regulations without any regard,

5. and carrying out activities that compete with the party and constitution, 6. and any disregard for the rules and laws of the country from the date the constitution comes into effect in that country, the list is not exhaustive. 7. The disciplinary policy means everyone must be heard if they appeal within four weeks and is entitled to a meeting where the party leader or the disciplinary committee or any appointed member can hear the case with the party leader informed and issuing the final decision. The individual concerned can choose to be accompanied by a friend or any

member to be appointed by the party members responsible for the meeting. The person where the case is complicated can choose to appeal to the global leaders who will make the final decision. Their decision is final, and no further appeal is available after that. The leadership depending on circumstances can inform the person to rejoin after a certain period say minimum 3 months as long as the case was not very serious but the person if he or she had a party officer role and where there are issues of trust must not rejoin the management team but can be an ordinary member.

29. CREATION OF A MEMBERSHIP BUFFER ACCOUNT.

1. A Membership Buffer Account must be set up where funds are kept in this account to cover for those who still want to be members but cannot pay the membership. 2. Such people need to send their names to the membership secretary.

3. No one shall leave the party due to the failure to pay membership fees. Anyone who has not paid for membership for three months will have their membership paid from this account automatically.

4. But failure to pay for a year without pointing to financial difficulties can lead the membership secretary or committee to regard such a membership as ceased.

5. The member's personal digital wallet account initially with 1000 FCI our digital currency will act as collateral for Tomorrow's World Order to provide a loan to that person for membership purposes.

6. The Buffer Account will work based on the fact that we will hold digital savings accounts of all members as their digital wallets which we will use as collateral to exempt membership fees for certain periods and to pay for the membership of that member but the equivalent value to be deducted at the end when the member

wishes to withdraw from the digital account.

7. Every member has access to these 1000 FCIs upon paying the membership

registration fee to be set by the party leader or the National Executive Power.

Initially £10 for ordinary membership, and £20 for Founding membership.

8. Payments can be made to our PayPal account:

9. Paypal.me/Tomorrowsworldorder

30. TYPES OF MEMBERSHIP

31. FOUNDING MEMBERS.

1. Have different statuses, rights and privileges and the subscription fees are slightly higher but can apply for roles without the qualifying period.

2. Are automatic members of the National and Ultimate Executive Power and votes at the National Congress. Can take up Parliament roles. They can

represent the party globally and can choose to work in branches in other countries. Normally involved in strategic planning, contribution, etc. of the expansion strategy.

3. They can be selected to be directors for the Tomorrow's World Order registered company governed by the Companies Act, the company exists to provide a steady income for the political party donating to the party

according to the law.

4. We aim to help new rising political leaders among the party and the

company can sponsor or donate political funds for campaigning to the top leaders and as such no Founding members can be entitled to that sponsorship. 5. But grants to aspiring leaders are from Tomorrow's World Order Global who will create a separate grants-fund-account for this purpose.

32. FULL MEMBERS
1. Are general party members who have paid the subscription and can vote as long as they are regarded as active members.

2. But must wait and qualify first before taking roles and might not go for the top job etc. Normally need to be a fully paying member for a minimum of 3 months to apply for administrative roles and 6 months to apply for party roles.

3. Can't be directors of Tomorrow's World Order Ltd but might donate to the company.

4. Might also qualify for the sponsorship or donation from the company Tomorrow's World Order Ltd for

political campaigns or career.

33. ASSOCIATED MEMBERS
1. Some people become members in the sense because they are employed by us and are not members in the sense, so they have no voting rights etc. Most are in administrative roles.

34. ARTICLE 5

35. FINANCIAL MANAGEMENT AND FUNDING ARRANGEMENTS
(NB if not mentioned all references to the Treasurer

means David Gomadza)

1. The survival of the political party depends to some extent on how we maintain our financial records. Maintaining integrity and grandparents is paramount. Credibility is important in politics. People, especially party funders and donors need to have confidence so a proper system and

standardized procedures must be in place.

2. Need for advanced safeguards to be in place and procedures to be in place for accountability purposes.

Funding Arrangements

1. We intend to comply with the requirements of the PPERA in making sure that we only accept donations and loans and other sources of income from permissible sources only meaning we have safeguards and arrangements in place with the party's Treasurer (David Gomadza) responsible to carry out extensive checks to make sure we comply with the requirements of the

PPERA.

2. This means that the party's Treasurer (David Gomadza) or any appointed or delegated member as authorized will be obliged by the party to carry out exhaustive checks with regard to all received donations and loans checking that.

3. The donors are permissible, meaning that they are based in the UK if donated money or given loans are over £500.

4. Any amount above £500 must be treated in accordance with the

requirements of the PPERA making sure that the donor's name and address is recorded and checked if the donor or loan lender is UK based. The value of the donation and whether the same donor or lender has donated before.

5. The party has safeguards in place to make sure we comply with the requirements of the PPERA, and these are assigning the role to the party Treasurer (David Gomadza) to continuously check if received funds are from permissible donors who are based in UK and meaning that they are on the voters register and are able to vote with their registered address based in UK.

6. Most of our donations are received through online sources and via PayPal as this method is the one to be used to collect registered members' contributions, meaning small amounts from several sources of around 30 pounds.

7. The party will require all donations from users that have declared themselves as registered and declared their home address with PayPal. All PayPal users must be all registered meaning that they must declare that they are on the electoral register and are able to vote within the UK.

8. We have safeguards in place to make sure that our credit card system will make sure that the donor's address will match that of the billing or registered address with the bank. Any shift from this means the donation will be rejected automatically.

9. The treasurer to continuously checks that we only receive permissible donations and loans. This is mandatory and a critical requirement. 10. Further we have other safeguards in place that will notify all potential

donors or lenders NOT to donate unless they are qualified to do so. Meaning that they must be able to vote in the UK and must have a registered address that is based in the UK. Our website has a message informing potential donors only to donate if they can meet these requirements and all our materials will have the same warning message.

11. The party Treasurer will check to make sure that we comply with the UK laws by checking where donations are from, corporations that are based and operating in the UK, meaning carrying business in the UK.

12. The treasurer if discovered that we accepted impermissible donations must within 30 days return that donation and record and report it as per PPERA requirements.

13. The treasurer must record sources of all donations and report those above £500 including any loans received and must send loan reports every quarter on the 30th of April, July, September, and January.

OUR MAIN SOURCES OF FUNDING.
1. Mass membership type. Grassroots funding: membership funds received via PayPal and online and these must be fees of less than £30 collected from those who are to be registered with us. This must be our major source of income as we aim to collect over 75% of all our donations this way.

2. That includes collections of monthly subscriptions, gifts, and dues etc. 3. Other donations from individuals who are wealthy must be checked and recorded and reported depending on the value.

4. Our other source of income is from corporations' donations. We have safeguards in place to check using our credit card system to check if the corporations are registered in the UK and if they operate their business in the UK.

5. The Treasurer again mandated to check if donations are above 500 pounds, if the corporation is registered and operating in UK and report

this. If the company is impermissible then the donations to be returned and this reported to the PPERA.

6. When receiving loans the Treasurer must enter the name, address of lender, company registration, the time period of the loan, the date the loan taken, the interest to be repaid, value of the loan, the interest rate, check also if the lender is UK based, record and report. All loans over 7500 pounds to be recorded and reported and these include any additional loans amounting to 1500 pounds from the same source.

7. The treasurer to adhere to all requirements of the PPERA in relation to reporting, accepting, and returning loans as stipulated in the Act.

Funding Arrangements between Tomorrow's World Order Ltd registration number 12326946 and the party Tomorrow's World Order.

(A quick point to note here; initially we had saw it fit to form and register a Foundation namely Tomorrow's World Order Party Foundation that was to fund aspiring individuals through career development grants so that we have the best leaders out there but we abandoned the idea because of the legality and operation of the Foundation that is based on donations left in Wills as legacy money something we are fighting to stop. We believe all wealth to be left with the deceased's relatives rather than governments. Therefore, the funding of future leaders will now be the sole responsibility of Tomorrow's World Order Global that is still based in the UK meaning compliance with the PPERA requirements.) We will establish a global office also in the UK.

1. Firstly Tomorrow's World Order Ltd hereon referred to as the company is registered in the UK registration number 12326946 under the companies act 2006 and its Memorandum of Association will govern its operation and how it deals with donations according

to UK statutory law.

2. The company, since it is based in the UK, will donate to the party in accordance with the law and this money is recorded and reported as well.

3. Purpose of the company; is to invest funds sourced from donations and loans from the UK and with the proceeds the profit from investment then donates to the party.

4. The Treasurer to make sure that donations to the party directly are not categorized and channeled as ' capital' for the company so as to maintain transparency and integrity.

5. The company can be funded by Tomorrow's World Order Global as long as the donations are within the stipulated limits.

6. The company can organize and hold meetings, campaigns etc. and directly fund expenditure directly linked to these meetings, conferences etc.

7. The other main role of the company is to publish material for the party, especially books, manuals etc. written by the party leader and donate the proceeds to the party as within UK statutory law.

Funding arrangements between Tomorrow's World Order Global and Tomorrow's World Order UK.

1. Tomorrow's World Order Global can and must fund individual aspiring party leaders through personal grants that are for the development and training of the aspiring party leaders.

2. Donations can be made to individual members as grants to give access to all, especially the disadvantaged, so that they have equal chances of being elected.

3. All this must be within the statutory framework of the law of

that country.

4. To avoid donations from the global party regarded as foreign contributions the amount donated must meet the statutory requirements for a given period and the global party will have a local presence as well.

Other Sources Of Donations And Loans.
1. The party may secure funds from other sources as long as the corporations, for example, are operating within the UK. The party leader I David Gomadza owns a publishing company that operates in the United Kingdom publishing several books and any donations from these is still to be treated as donations from unincorporated corporations etc. based and operated within the UK therefore within the statutory requirements.

2. In the long run we can raise funding from other ventures like digital currency's implementation and use but any income from these is through a registered company and again we rely on the requirements of the PPERA and treat this money as donations from corporations registered or unincorporated but still based in the UK registered with the Companies House.

3. It is the Treasurer's party's mandate to check that all sources of donations and loans are within the permissible criteria, meaning that individuals must be able to vote and are registered. If companies must then be registered in the UK and operate in the UK. If unincorporated associations, they must carry out business or other activities in the UK.

4. The role of the Treasurer to iron out any issues and inconsistencies, if any, that might arise in the foreseeable future regarding findings, especially considering that we are introducing a new system of governance.

5. There are safeguards to be put in place with a role created once a

party is formed for a compliance officer answerable to the party Treasurer, but the Treasurer remains as the main person and responsible person tasked with making sure that we adhere to the requirements of the PPERA.

6. A system to be put in place that removes the risks of accepting illegal money. All foreign donations are to be made to Tomorrow's World Order Global and not to Tomorrow's World Order UK.

7. Checks to ensure that any funding from Tomorrow's World Order is directly linked to the development of the individual and is for training and personal development rather than funding the UK party.

8. The Treasurer was tasked with assessment of permissibility and other statutory requirements.

16

9. Tomorrow's World Order UK is a subsidiary of Tomorrow's World Order Global. The global party will still have offices in the United.

Kingdom and still based in the UK even though it covers other countries but still will observe the statutory requirements as stipulated in the

PPERA.

10. The Treasurer to deny and return any underhand or unreported

donations.

Other links and collaborations with other organizations etc.

1. Following the statutory requirements in the PPERA act we can accept contributions and donations in kind from other sources. We can work.

with other publishing agencies like the company owned by the party

leader who produces books that have themes related to our party goals.

and who can sell the books to our registered members as publication?

materials to raise awareness of the pressing issues. But any of these are to be accepted as donations or contributions as per the requirements of

the PPERA. We can collaborate with others but still the Treasurer must make sure that the donations or contributions follow the requirements of the PPERA.

The Proposed Financial Scheme.

1. Our financial scheme is consistent with the Constitution and in line with the requirements of the PPERA in that all our dealings are in

according to the Act.

2. It is the duty of the Treasurer to have the final check and verification that all our operations are within the law.

3. The Treasurer mandated to ensure integrity and transparency of

political party finance by ensuring that safeguards are in place to check and verify continuously and to amend, record and report any.

inconsistencies and plan for these by establishing a contingency.

team to ensure that the party is acting in accordance with the law. If

online income e.g., PayPal check if registered users are able to vote and within the UK. Any foreign incomes above the limit must be donated to the

Global account rather than the UK branch. The Treasurer is mandated to safeguard this and check matching of billing addresses to home addresses etc.

4. All the safeguards will see us comply and act within UK law.

36. TOMORROW'S WORLD ORDER'S FINANCIAL SCHEME

1. In order to meet the requirements of the Political Parties Electoral Referendum Act 2000 we have adopted the Financial Scheme in appendix Article 20 detailing the required tasks and we shall rely on this Financial Scheme as having fulfilled the requirements of the Acts.

2. The appointment and assigning of the party Treasurer [David Gomadza or one to be appointed] as the official person to be registered with the commission as the person

responsible to meet the requirements of the Act and designating an office at the

Headquarters and giving them the power to further appoint a Financial Committee to deal with all day-to-day aspects means meeting the requirements of the PPERA.

3. We have a detailed systematic standardized plan we adopted as a political party to organize the financial aspect of the party in order to systematically collect, record, monitor, audit, investigate, publish, and report our financial status to the relevant body as required by the Political Parties Electoral

Referendum Act 2000. We shall use the standardization procedures.

assigning a role and an office at the Headquarters of the Treasurer [David Gomadza] who must register with the commission and who will be.

responsible and accountable to make sure that we comply with the

requirements of the PPERA.

4. The National Executive Power and the Party leader to appoint a Treasurer and assign tasks to meet compliance with the PPERA.

5. He or she shall be responsible for adopting a standardized procedure to make sure things are in place to meet the requirements of the PPERA.

6. He shall appoint a Financial Committee and task it with this task with him acting as the authorization authority.

7. A detailed workflow plan with roles and individuals, with deadlines written clearly on the chart with the plan approved by the Party Leader. Bylaws can be created to detail the process and standardize it.

8. Clear calendar dates [1 January to 31 December] as the financial year must be noted with everyone knowing when the political financial year starts and ends. Reporting dates marked with an external audit from outside the

committee responsible for inspecting before documents are sent. In addition to the duties and roles in the adopted Financial Scheme, the Treasurer shall record all financial transactions of income and expenditure detailing,

donations, loans, contributions, expenses, etc. providing a detailed account or making sure that the elected committee shall comply with the auditing and authorizing.

9. The Party Leader or members of the disciplinary committee can become proactive and audit in advance to check, especially after first establishing the branch with drills to make sure the system and standardization process is fit for purpose. Failure to comply triggers the disciplinary process see Article 12. 10. The Treasurer on approval by the Party leader and or the National

Executive Power can appoint other accounting units if needed to make sure that the party complies with the requirements of the Act. Bylaws can be.

created using the party's procedure in this constitution.

37. ARTICLE 6

38. POLICY DEVELOPMENT

1. This is one area critical and related to the voter's supporters and is able to influence voters and turn people towards the party.

2. Greater importance is therefore placed on the processes with everything standardized.

3. A National Policy Committee must be established, and it is the duty of the National Executive Power to appoint one or facilitate its development.

4. The global Ultimate Executive Power and the global Party leader can and must strategically plan and assign the National Executive Powers to establish National Policy Committees.

39. NATIONAL POLICY COMMITTEE
1. Aims and objectives are to make policy development happen.

2. To identify potential critical policy areas and choose which policies to forward for discussions.

3. Identify areas for research and order the research before

arranging conferences to discuss the researched topic before recommending to the National

Executive Power, The Ultimate Executive Power, and the Global Party

Leader.

4. Coordinate the policy development platform.

5. Can conduct reviews of policies

6. Members mostly are appointed by the above powers, and some are visitors from around the country, experts in certain areas who contribute voluntarily and are interested in solving issues.

7. The Committee must have a chairperson deputy and a secretary.

8. Experts to be employed or invited to participate, especially those with much experience in policy formulation and development.

40. RULES AND PROCEDURES REGARDING NATIONAL POLICY COMMITTEE
1. The National Executive Power or the Ultimate Executive Power, when they first hold their conference, they must also appoint or establish a National Policy Committee.

2. The committee is answerable to the National Executive and liaises with the Party leader as well.

41. THE POLICY FORMULATION PROCESS.
1. Tomorrow's World Order UK even if it is guided by Tomorrow's

World Order's broader goals the party has a plan and program to

decide what issues to address locally.

2. The local party UK shall hold conference meetings more often to decide issues that matter to them, and issues raised to be voted and any two

thirds majority will see that issue form the local manifesto.

3. The Party Leader and the National Executive Power and all other local units shall be involved in policy formulation asking members to forward issues that matter to them and these ranked and voted for.

4. The chosen topic shall then form the elements of the manifesto.

42. MAINTAINING INDIVIDUAL AUTONOMY AND MAINTAINING DIVERSITY AS A GOAL.
1. While Tomorrow's World Order aims to broaden the scope of us

activities globally, we also believe in individual autonomy.

2. We aim to maintain nations as they are. Protecting the customs and practices of Britain.

3. This means protecting and strengthening Britain's borders.

4. Controlling immigration and preserving what is British.

43. POWERS OF T.W.O [UK]
1. To achieve our goals and objectives and within the framework of the law in carrying out our activities the party shall have powers too.

2. Fundraise and seek donations from anyone who qualifies as governed by the Political Parties Electoral Referendum Act 2000 and to accept those donations; recording these as stipulating by the governing body; keeping all records for reporting to the PPERA at the time we are required reporting.

3. To raise any contributions and receive these according to the

rules and regulations.

4. To seek, accept and receive the fees in relation to the joining of our party and subscription fees and to register all those on our register who have shown interest and commitment to join us and be governed by our laws and regulations. A register of which we will keep and one that members will have an excess to, and one which other can request in writing to

the membership secretary or anyone delegated at the time.

5. We as T.W.O [UK] have the power to publish materials in line with our aims and objectives which we will use for campaigning and for fulfilling our objectives. Material we can distribute free or for a fee, material we can publish in any format and to anyone around the globe and material which will contain our core values and principles, therefore, materials that belong to T.W.O [UK] and on behalf of T.W.O [Global].

6. We shall have powers to select and elect people through the party leader, Secretary, and the National Executive Power to various positions within our party and to employ and pay these people we see fit as they help in the running of the party as long as it is within the guiding principles of the laws of the country concerned and globally as a whole.

7. We as T.W.O [UK] and T.W.O [Global] have the power to open bank accounts for the sake of carrying out our activities and to purchase and

make payments for infrastructure and other consumables as long as

Everything is for the purpose of fulfilling our objectives as guided by the constitution. That means we can acquire and run, lease, rent and or sell buildings.

8. We have the power to take out insurances for the sake of

carrying out our duties and to use the extra cash we might have accumulated to be put to good use through investing these in accordance with other applicable laws e.g., the Trustee laws.

9. We can carry out any activities we see fit as long as they are according to law; to plan, to obtain services and resources we need, and this can mean entering into contracts to get real estate or personal property with the aim of fulfilling our objectives. This can also mean us following the rules and

regulations of the UK and other nation's Companies Acts as we have.

register our party as a Private Company limited by guarantee without

share capital etc. Reg number 12326946 as Tomorrow's World Order LTD

44. CONTRACTUAL LIABILITY
1. Only authorized party officials can and must authorize or enter a

contract for property and assets with any external forces and in most cases a designated person or committee e.g., the Financial Committee can do that.

45. ARTICLE 7

46. THE STRUCTURE

47. GLOBAL LEVEL

48. ULTIMATE PARTY LEADER [GLOBAL PRESIDENT] DUTIES.
1. Founder and President or global party leader.

2. To set the direction the party will take.

3. Must write laws, the constitution and involved in policy development

49. ULTIMATE EXECUTIVE POWER
Duties.

1. They must.

2. Check to see if the party leader is implementing policies according to the

constitution.

3. Recommends, advise, checklist, involved in decision making, policy development, and analysis,

4. Hold meetings to check progress, review policies, determine expansion strategy, advise, recommend, and check if the global leader is implementing policy as agreed in meetings and as per the constitution.

50. NATIONAL LEVEL
51. PARTY OR NATIONAL CONFERENCE
 Duties.

1. Must be involved in governing at the national level. The supreme governing unit at the national level

2. Their decisions are bidding on all

3. But answerable to the Ultimate Executive Power and the global leader,

4. Must approve amendments and rectifications to the constitution and other statutes.

5. Must be responsible for the selection of Party Leaders at the national level or arranging the voting system for the selection.

6. At the national level the Party's highest body.

7. Must hold meetings at least every two years.

8. Must elect members of the National Executive at their first meeting.

9. Must elect most committees and commission

10. Must liaise with the Ultimate Executive Power and the Global President

11. Must be responsible for approving rules and in bylaw formulations approving candidates for selection, amending the constitution and in financial management. 12. To stipulate how many delegates from various structures can be part of this

Conference.

13. To determine notice periods before the Conference, the voting process, and the quorum

14. To determine or facilitate national policy formulation.

Composition.

1. If in power or expanded well enough must consist of more than 500

delegates from all over the country.

2. Consist of the.

3. National Party Leader and the vice-presidents

4. Party Executive

5. Government members

6. Representative from other external bodies

7. Representatives from all lower-level branches

8. Five to ten delegates from the Women's League

9. Three to five delegates from the Youth League

10. A system of proportional representation can be used to select delegates through a single ballot with affirmative action.

11. The selection and election of delegates must be carried out a year before the date of the Conference.

12. National Executive to arrange the National Conference and should be held every two to three years.

13. A special National Conference can be arranged at any time and a notice of four weeks can be given.

14. When in power the President and Vice President attend the Conference with full rights but have no voting rights as they are not delegates.

15. The National Secretary is not a delegate as well and lacks voting rights

16. The National Secretary to determine the agenda of the conference.

17. He or she shall give three months' notice to everyone to send policy topics to be discussed to the National Policy Committee.

52. NATIONAL EXECUTIVE
1. To meet more frequently than at the Conference and cover the Conference the times when it is not holding meetings.

2. To report and is answerable to the Conference as well as the party leader.

3. They might call for a special conference called an Extraordinary Conference if needed.

4. Must carry out the party's administrative duties.

5. The National Conference can elect at least thirty members as executives. 6. Includes the National President, Vice President, Secretary, etc.

7. National Executive to use proportional representation to fill seats

8. Includes leaders and representatives from all lower branches.

9. Must have at least ten members from the Women's League.

10. Must have three to five or more from the Youth League.

11. Must have delegates from all other committees; the Policy, Finance, Standing, etc.

12. All their decisions are binding on all.

13. Answerable to National Conferences.

 Must be responsible for administrative duties like; 1. Carrying out the directives of the National Conference.

2. Must interpret the constitution if requested to.

3. Must clarify issues arising from the constitution.

4. Must direct all members to the lower branches.

5. Must call for a special National Conference according to the rules stipulated above, giving three months' notice etc.

6. Must respond to the request of all national branches who might request special tasks etc.

7. Must elect most of the committee forming bylaws to govern these committees e.g., the National Policy, The Standing Committee.

8. Must address matters brought to them by all including from the Women and Youth Leagues.

9. To hear appeals from lower branches and might delegate such tasks. 10. After hearing appeals they can overturn the decision of the lower states and replace it with their own or must request the lower-level branch to reconsider the case again or can choose a different branch to re-examine that case.

11. If lower branches are not following the constitution or in error the National Executive can take over the branch or appoint new members to oversee the branch.

12. Must meet at least three times a year.

13. Must delegate the convening of meetings to the National Executive Committee.

14. Can meet through telephoning conferencing if need be or video conferencing. 15. Resolution to be given in person or in writing and all are binding.

53. THE NATIONAL EXECUTIVE COMMITTEE.
1. This takes over or operates at the time when the National Executive Power is not in operation.

2. Must carry out all administrative duties

3. Implementing and checking tasks given by the National Executive Power. 4. Shall meet in between the two meetings of the National Executive Power. 5. The purposes of the meetings are to prepare agendas to be discussed at the National Executive Power meeting.

6. Must follow all the notice rules requesting topics to be discussed as the policy to be sent to the National Policy Committee.

7. To arrange meetings and give four weeks' notice, choosing the venue and time and responsible for the smooth running of the meetings.

8. To note topics of policy to be discussed at the National Executive.

9. Must not replace the National Executive Power nor make decisions in their place but only facilitate or prepare the agendas to be discussed at the

National Executive Power.

10. The National Executive to acknowledge the work of the National Executive Committee and endorse this when they hold their meeting.

54. NATIONAL PARTY LEADER.
 Duties.

1. To represent the party

2. Party members to directly elect the National Party leaders a year before the National Conference.

3. A single ballot with proportional representation and affirmative action to be used to elect the party leader and two [senior and junior] presidents can be elected.

4. They have a year in office in those positions.

5. The role is to lead the National Conference meetings and those of the National Executive Power.

6. He or she is answerable to the National Executive and executes

their decisions. They also monitor if he or she is implementing policies as agreed in meetings and according to the policy.

55. REGIONAL BRANCHES

1. To follow the same procedures to establish these everywhere necessary.

56. LOCAL BRANCHES

1. To be established according to the constitution and local bylaws.

57. THE WOMEN'S LEAGUE.

1. The National Executive must establish or facilitate the creation of a Women's League.

2. As a general rule, all women registered as members of the party automatically qualify to join.

3. There is no membership fee.

4. Duties.

5. Must encourage women to join and participate in policy development and decision making.

6. Must act as a recruitment drive.

7. Must aim to spread messages about party values and principles.
8. Must act to train others and improve skills and positions obtained by women through sponsorship and work experience programs etc.

9. Must formulate an agenda to be discussed at the National Women's league. Sending notice 3 months between the National Women's League.

10. Must be answerable to the National Women's League and must implement the directives of this league.

11. Must provide links between the party and the communities.

12. Must represent the party to the outside world.

13. To provide, nominate and elect women who will become representative of the national regional and Global Women's Forums.

58. YOUTH LEAGUES

1. The National Executive must establish or facilitate the creation of a

Youth's League.

2. Open to youths of any age.

3. No membership fees.

4. Aim to create future dedicated party leaders and members.

5. To spread messages about the party.

6. Involved in policy formulation.

7. Must represent the party to the outside world.

8. To appoint Youth representatives globally.

59. THE PARTY'S DECISION-MAKING PROCESS

1. This part deals with the party's decision-making process.

2. The leader or President of the Tomorrow's World Order Global is the ultimate decision-making person, but he is answerable to the Ultimate Executive Power Board that also has powers to make, correct, suggest, and recommend decisions.

3. At a national level, the party leader or President is responsible for the overall decision-making process, but he is also answerable to a National Executive Power Board who acts to check, verify,

recommend, liaise, suggest, etc. and work with this leader to make sure that the party objectives can be realized.

4. The general quorum for meetings is seven.

5. Annual general meetings are compulsory for all with special, and extraordinary meetings called upon when needed, etc.

6. For all meetings, two weeks' notice is needed, and communication is by post or electronic.

60. ROLE OF THE ULTIMATE EXECUTIVE POWER PARTY LEADER

1. This is the highest office of Tomorrow's World Order. At the moment it is held by the founder me [David Gomadza] and the Ultimate President of Tomorrow's World Order.

2. The Roles.

3. As the founder of the political party; laying down the fundamental

principles and rules to be followed and to write down the constitution.

clearly stating the objectives of the party as a whole on a global scale.

4. To lay the foundation and basis and the core founding principles of

Tomorrow's World Order.

5. Has powers to define the path the party will follow.

6. Is the authorizing authority for any amendments and any rectification or addition to the constitutions, rules, new systems, and procedures. Most of the changes require [my] signature as the

leader unless the task has been delegated to another member before such a time when any Ultimate Executive Leader can do so.

7. Very active role in making sure that members take control and leadership in all nations on earth starting with the first seven nations, followed by the next 24 nations and then the 42 nations with the aim of putting members

peacefully of course through contesting in parliamentary elections globally in leadership roles in order to realize the plan of implementing a brand-new system of global governance, fiscal monitoring, planning and management and the judiciary system.

8. Has tasks to invent, draft, design, put things in place, implement, monitor, and follow up to introduce a completely new system of global governance that will eliminate all today's global problems and take humanity to new heights.

9. Liaise with the current leadership pitching them on our new system and how this will benefit all mankind.

10. Form partnerships and links.

11. Write new laws and books laying the principles and rules to be adhered to. 12. Appointing bodies to implement the new global system.

13. Appoint members who form the Ultimate Executive Power; the Ultimate Judiciary Power and the Ultimate Legislative Power.

14. Appoint the new judiciary posts to implement and enforce the new system. 15. To appoint a project leader responsible for all global projects, designing, planning, and building of the Global Reserve Bank, etc.

61. PROJECT IMPLEMENTATION AND DEVELOPMENT PLAN.

1. The Ultimate Executive Power to appoint a Project Leader who will assemble a team that will be responsible for the overall implementation of all projects, financial, fiscal, judiciary, governing, infrastructural, political, etc. in all countries.

2. These will see the successful implantation of the new system of governance throughout the world.

62. THE FUTURE STRUCTURE OF THE ULTIMATE EXECUTIVE POWER.

1. When the implementation has taken place, the Ultimate Executive Power will comprise two Ultimate Executive Power Presidents with equal powers meaning two equal [twin power] global Presidents. With the other

Presidents acting as the equal yet opposing power suggesting alternatives but working together.

2. This will also consist of twenty-four national executive presidents

representing their nations on a global scale. They will carry out the same duties together helping, the two Ultimate Executive Presidents to

implement, enforce, monitor, alter and amend the constitution, the judiciary laws, the legislative laws, etc.

3. The founder the Ultimate Executive President shall select and nominate the second Ultimate President but if the twenty-four National Executive

members have already taken their positions then they all shall vote in order to elect the second Ultimate President. If there is a tie, then the Ultimate Executive President shall cast the deciding vote.

The member winning by the majority shall be appointed as the President.

4. When the number of leaders of Tomorrow's World Order representing us in all nations reaches forty-two the Ultimate Executive Power President can become seven having the highest office all working together. These seven can then choose who will be their leader too among them.

63. FUTURE ROLE OF THE NATIONAL PARTY LEADER
1. The party leader shall represent the party's views and objectives nationally and globally.

2. The constitution to meet the requirements of the PPERA requires the Party Leader to be registered with the relevant bodies and the structure through charts and workflow must show who is the leader and define his duties and who he or she is answerable to if any. This constitution gives powers to the Ultimate or National Executive Power to act on behalf of the party to verify the duties of the Party leader and recommend or approval of his or her acts. They must check more often if the Party Leader is doing everything to make sure the party goals are achieved. It checks to see if the agreed policies etc. are being implemented by the party leader as agreed.

3. Act as an opposing voice to veto some decisions if they are not in line with the constitution.

4. Overall must work well with Party bodies to realize the party goals.

5. Must contest elections with the aim of winning and getting into the highest political office of the country concerned.

6. Assess the feasibility of implementing our new system. Assess the obstacles and challenges and invent, develop, and plan for

solutions.

7. Has duties to see that the party will achieve its objectives of getting elected and winning the elections in order for the party to fulfill and realize its

goals.

8. Advocate for the party's values to everyone.

9. Managing the party's business; proposing and developing strategies to be considered and evaluated by the National Executive Power.

10. Involved in the implementation of the strategies approved by the National Executive Power.

11. To liaise with the Chairperson and the National Executive Power on challenging strategies formulating party policy.

12. Must be the communication piece pitching to potential supporters,

members, donors, contributors, and other people of interest who might help the party to achieve its goals.

13. Responsible for managing the members, making sure to some extent that the constitution complies with several other laws and regulations even though this is the duty of the compliance officer whom he can appoint.

14. Duties to implement the constitution and spearhead the party in the right direction.

15. Doing his or her best to make sure that the party will win the parliamentary elections.

16. Involved in policy development, communication, and

implementation. 17. Vetoing and refusal of some laws and rules.

18. Shall enforce the constitution and see that all activities are in line with the constitution.

19. Responsible for the appointment of the Treasurer and the members of the National Executive Power.

20. Responsible for appointing a party chairperson and his or her deputy who if he or she is not around shall take over the proceedings of the meeting. If both are available, the deputy shall assume the leadership roles for the sake of the meeting.

21. Shall act as the authorizing authority at the national level to give the final say when amendments to the constitution and bylaws are needed, signing off documents, etc.

22. In case the party is in government the party leader shall act according to carrying out parliamentary duties as required.

23. Appointing people in different positions as MPs or the shadow cabinet. 24. Shall assign people in different roles forming his cabinet as he or she sees fit.

25. Holding parliamentary meetings, conferences, and debates as required and according to the constitution and all other laws representing Tomorrow's World Order.

26. Making the decision to run the country in line with our global goals to bring wealth to all.

27. Must liaise with the Global leader at least once a year but overall shall act with the interest of the United Kingdom in mind advancing its goals and maintaining its national autonomy.

28. Shall implement our new governance and financial system at the national level.

64. ELECTION OF THE PARTY LEADER

1. The Ultimate Executive Power can nominate party leaders for national posts initially and subsequently these can be elected and nominated through the voting system.

2. The party leader shall be elected to the role through voting by members whose subscriptions are up to date and are on the member's list. The candidate with the most votes shall become the leader and every member shall have a single vote. Potential candidate names are forwarded to the National Executive Power who will arrange the conference for voting.

inviting all eligible members to attend and cast a vote.

3. Elections can be called for when a party leader dies, resigns, or is voted out of office, etc. The National Executive Power shall call for an election within three months to replace that leader through voting. The National Executive Power must in the event of resignation or death hold elections within a month to replace the party leader.

4. They also have the power to elect an acting replacement within two weeks after the event until a new party leader is elected.

65. TERM IN OFFICE

1. The party leader shall have four years in office as a leader. Extensions can be agreed upon by the National Executive Power who shall decide for how long and normally for no more than two more years.

66. ROLE OF THE CHAIRPERSON

1. He is employed by the Party Leader.

2. He can act as well as the Compliance officer who is there to make sure that the constitution of Tomorrow's World Order is in

compliance with the

requirements of the PPERA, the Equality Act and the Human Rights Acts, etc. making sure everything does not conflict with these laws unless if a specific Compliance officer is already appointed.

3. In that case, he has to liaise with all including the Party Leader to make sure that everything is okay. If not okay; to arrange for rectifications informing the Party Leader or any appointed member within a specified time frame.

4. Takes the role of the leader when the leader is not available; needs initial approval though.

5. To encourage links and liaising of all members encouraging constructive debate.

6. To ensure that all the Executive Power's policies are in the interest of the party.

7. To act as a checklist performer to make sure that the recommendations of the National Executive Power are implemented by the Party Leader.

8. To sit in meetings noting the agenda and noting the important issues and making sure that these are discussed by the Executive Power.

9. To check and maintain the highest standards and make sure that the constitution, the bylaws, etc. all comply, etc.

67. ARTICLE 8

68. THE PARTY'S PROCEDURAL RULES

1. Tomorrow's World Order constitution places requirements and rules to be observed and used to act as guiding principles that will

make it easy for the party to comply with all requirements.

2. As a general rule, procedural aspects must be followed.

3. This means meeting all the statutory requirements. This must be the duty of the Statutory Compliance officer.

4. All procedures must be followed, and a plan put in place to checklist that. Standard documentation to be used to produce reports that check e.g., that the Party leader's name is registered with the Electoral Commission.

5. That person must also check if the Electoral Commission has acknowledged the receipt and amends the party's documentation.

6. A designated officer must also make sure that all bodies like the National Executive Power and other committees as they grow to a certain number a procedural officer must make sure also to comply with the Equality and

Human Rights Acts etc.

7. If the National Executive reaches a certain number say 40 a certain number of these must be women minimum say a third or more.

8. A certain number must be of certain ethnic backgrounds etc. e.g., one for every ten.

9. The voting system shall be used to appoint and elect members to different positions. The majority rule to be adopted with two-thirds deciding the vote. 10. Requirements on the voting candidates to be used like only qualified members to vote.

11. Qualified means active members who have paid the subscription fees. 12. Depending on the size of the party and as the National Executive Power and the Leader see fit, they might

authorize the formation of branches and

subsidiaries and other groups like the Youth Branch to involve the young. 13. They can authorize the formation of the women's party, and this can also mean complying with the Equality laws.

14. As a general rule the bigger the party the more demands for other groups within the party.

15. The procedural rules shall become the basis to use to determine the

establishment and nomination of further groups, branches, etc.

16. Everyone shall be encouraged to participate fully without fear or intimidation and voting for things that matter and every suggestion to be considered for discussion and formulation into policy or manifesto.

69. ARTICLE 9
70. THE POLICY DEVELOPMENT PROCESS.
71. STANDARDS AND PROCEDURES

1. Standardization of procedures

2. Use the following guidelines to the creation of standardization,

documentation, and procedural aspects to make it easy and mandate to comply with the relevant reporting and operational laws as in PPERA.

3. Use Separation of Duties to,

4. Create and plan for a clear definition and plan those states who are responsible for what and when. Creating a workflow plan and a chart that is seen by all and distributing the information to all.

5. Use Access Controls,

6. Define who has access and to what. Define the levels of access held by each committee member and who to see if one has limited access. There must be a flow chart showing the access chart with links and names of who has what kind of access and to what information and who is above that access hierarchy and when and how to get access if needed.

7. Use Physical Audits,

8. Tomorrow's World Order's financial committee must draw a plan that shows what information is held in physical form and what assets e.g., money in the petty cash safe is available and must be accounted for and by who and when and how this is reported and to who?

9. The Financial Committee Must Standardize Documents.

10.Designing or ordering documents that will form the standard reporting system. A clear plan showing who is responsible for the documents in case some run out, who to complete what document and if they need verification of an authorizing signature, who to do that and when and not available who to take over.

11. Use Trial Balances.

12. A system must be in place to designate who and when they can rely on trial balance for reporting and compiling other documents. Periodic reconciliation is to be used to determine when and how and who will reconcile the books and balances and who to report to and if an authorization is needed to authorize the reports and sign them and who to do all that.

13. Use the Approval Authority.

14.The Financial Committee must appoint someone to act as the signing-off authority with duties to authorize the documents and processes. 15. The same person who will carry out the final audit or checks to make sure that all processes have been carried out according to the rules and procedures and that all this is in line with the Constitution and the rules and procedures of the country and as required by the PPERA. If that person is not around another option must be in place so that the deadline is met and that all documents meet the statutory requirements.

16.Establish and Define the Overseeing Body or Personnel. 17. The Financial Committee shall be the overseeing body to make sure there is compliance with the financial reporting laws. This is also responsible for monitoring the banking, insurance, real estate and in the managing of the securities of the party.

18.Deciding and informing the leader when to invest the party's funds which they don't need to use in the near future.

19.Delegation of Powers in Advance.

20. The leader of Tomorrow's World Order Party or the Treasurer can delegate some powers in advance, usually at the beginning of taking office to the Financial Committee giving them operating powers in relation to the constitution. The Financial Committee will have the power to correct and take any action to correct any financial issues without the need to be authorized as authorization will have already been given at the beginning. They must see the overall financial aspect of the party budgeting, planning, monitoring, controlling, and reporting all these.

21. Assign A Party Treasurer.

22.The party Treasurer shall be responsible for the Financial Committee and for reporting of financial statement purposes the Treasurer shall be the Approving authority, auditing and check listing documents before signing them and sending them to the

Electoral Commission.

23. The Treasurer must be appointed by the party leader and shall be in office for two to three years.

24. He or she can resign, be voted off or dismissed by the leader.

25. All resignation shall be in writing giving a two weeks' notice and handed to the Secretary or in his absence to any member of the National Executive Power who will forward the resignation to the Secretary or even President or party leader who will first negotiate to keep the person; if not to wish him or her farewell and arrange voting for a replacement and or appoint someone else within two weeks of resignation date, etc.

72. ARTICLE 10
73. HIGHEST DECISION-MAKING BODIES
74. THE ULTIMATE EXECUTIVE POWER
1. This consists of.

2. The Ultimate Global Party Leader,

3. In the future- two Ultimate Global Party Leaders

4. A minimum group of seven country-specific Party Leaders that will rise to 24 leaders and then 42 leaders as more countries join in.

5. The Ultimate Secretary,

6. The Ultimate Treasurer,

7. The Head of Global.

8. Financial Committees,

9. Standing Committee,

10. Project Development and Implementation,

11. The Head of the Global Reserve Bank,

12. The Head of FutureGoldCoin,

13. The Head of all Multinational Companies,

14. The Head or Director of Tomorrow's World Order Ltd. 15. The list is not exhaustive.

75. THE NATIONAL EXECUTIVE POWER

1. Shall consists of the.

2. The Nation-specific Party Leader,

3. The Treasurer,

4. The Secretary,

5. The Chairperson,

6. The Deputy Chairperson,

7. The Nominating Officer

8. The Campaigner,

9. Other non-office holding members. A minimum of seven are required. 10. If any person, e.g., the leader holds one or more roles, some Party Officers of the party must be appointed and be present as members of the National Executive Power. The minimum number at any time must be seven even if the appointed ones have no specific titles.

11. All seven National Executive Power members have voting rights.

12. This is the National Executive Power that includes the Party leader who is the President as well.

13. Who will act as the Chairperson for the purposes of meetings who can delegate to his deputy or any party member?

14. There must also be a treasurer unless the leader is also the treasurer. The treasurer has an important role as the person responsible and required by the

law to maintain up-to-date financial statements and transactions of the party.

15. The National Executive Power is made up of the Secretary who can also be the leader and the Treasurer as long as another person will be there in

another role e.g., Nominating Officer or the Campaigner Officers.

76. ROLE OF THE NATIONAL EXECUTIVE POWER
1. The powers of these members among them are to see that T.W.O [UK] is operating within the confines of the constitution and the rules of the country they are operating to make sure that the party can and will fulfill its

objectives and aims as set out in the constitution.

2. They monitor all activities to make sure that the constitution is being followed and adhered to by all.

3. They are to put things in place, make amends, advance our vision to all, and advocate for our causes.

4. They hold and or delegate disciplinary meetings if no disciplinary committee exists.

5. They are involved in the day-to-day running of the party, calling for extraordinary meetings when needed, holding campaigns and meetings with the aim of achieving party goals.

6. They can link with other organizations with the same interest for

the purposes of carrying out their duties.

7. They can seek help from the global party on matters that are beyond their scope.

8. They represent the party in all the United Kingdom and globally as to advance the values of the party.

9. The National Executive Power together with the party leader has powers to manage the members and everyone including those who are employed by the party and in the managing of the party's assets. They are responsible for setting up offices, purchasing offices, renting, leasing, and the selling of purchased premises, etc. and with the help of the treasurer manage the party's funds efficiently and accurately.

10. The Executive Power has powers to approve parties' policies and manifestos in line with the constitutions.

11. They make the party leaders answerable to them for accountability purposes. 12. The Secretary, who is a member of the National Executive Power, has the main responsibility to maintain a register of all members, ensuring that every member is registered according to the constitution.

13. Maintaining the register and checking payments as well and informing the treasurer on the financial aspects.

14. The Secretary in line with the constitution can link with the Chairperson in arranging meetings, etc.

15. He or she can take notes and minutes of the meeting and make sure that any relevant important communications are passed to the members.

16. Through the party leader, the National Executive Power can amend, write, and correct the policies and rules of the Party at the

local level and can consult the global leadership in complicated matters.

17. They have all the powers to hold meetings, disciplinary meetings, organize and hold annual general meetings, make sure that the constitution is followed, make sure that the laws of the country are being adhered to and in line with

the constitution and take corrective action if not, managing the affairs of the party and representing Tomorrow's World Order in specific countries advancing our objectives.

77. ARTICLE 11

78. OFFICE BEARERS OF THE PARTY

1. The party has a structure and a hierarchy with everyone with a specific role put down in a workflow plan with a chart showing who does what as required by

specific laws with all these roles assigned to people and the structure written down so that anyone just needs access to party documents to know who to contact in case they need help, etc.

2. A clearly defined system with no ambiguity and in some cases with -on standby office bearers who will take over.

3. Some posts are to be appointed by the party leader and for some, the voting process is the method to be used.

4. Office bearers can resign by handing written notice with a two-week notice period in which the leader must find a temporary replacement within two weeks.

5. An election to be held four weeks after the resignation, death, or removal of the candidate.

6. If in conflict with the constitution or acting against it or

disregard other laws against recommendations of the constitution, the office-bearer's role can be

terminated in writing.

7. The person has the right to be heard, to appeal and can choose to bring a friend or choose an offered member of the party to represent him e.g., from another branch or country.

8. Appeals can be made to the appeals board or committee and must be made within four weeks of the notice.

9. The party leader can be appointed by the global leader or be elected through a voting system.

10. He has four years in office which can be extended by a further year or two. Most office bearers' posts have either a two year or just a year term in which new

members to be elected at the annual general meeting every year.

11. According to law the Secretary is responsible for the day-to-day running of the party and all correspondence must be chosen or appointed for and all laws complied with so that the Electoral Commission can be notified.

12. The National Executive, the Party Leader, the Ultimate Executive Power, or the Ultimate Leader must carry-out a checklist to make sure that the

following office bearers are appointed.

79. APPOINTING OF A STATUTORY COMPLIANCE OFFICER

1. Depending on the size of the party the constitution here gives provisions for the creation and appointment of a Statutory Compliance Officer who will act to make sure that the party as it

grows must comply with all the

statutory requirements.

2. This role must not be confused with that of the compliance office, but the role can be taken over by the Compliance office too.

3. Here this role entails concern with the procedural aspect of the laws rather than compliance with demands and requirements of the laws in terms of document provision.

4. This role means checking and or registering the roles of the Party Leader, the Secretary, and Nominating officer, etc.

80. THE POLITICAL PARTY AGENT.
1. Requirements of the laws of some countries you must appoint and designate a post and office at Headquarters for the position of the party agent, but the party agent must also have another office separate from the Headquarters.

2. This agent must be trusted with other party documents which he or she can keep away from Headquarters.

3. The person appointed must make links and liaise with a lot of external people and departments like MPS, government agencies and even foreign MEPs. 4. He or she must be a link to the outside of the party and must report to the party leader who represents the party to the outside world.

5. Must have a detailed workflow plan written and all the people he can liaise with be noted down.

6. The person must act as well as a compliance officer, ensuring that the party is complying with all electoral laws, etc.

7. He or she must represent the party where the party leader cannot and must complement the party leader's role rather than compete

with it.

8. He or she must have an office away from the headquarters and be given some documents as well he or she can keep at his or her office.

9. He or she can be neutral politically but must agree with our objectives and goals to a certain extent.

81. THE TREASURER.
1. The national laws of some countries make it a must to have a treasurer who will report and submit all required legal documents and the financial status of the party.

2. You must appoint and designate a post and an office at the Headquarters for the Treasurer. This will ensure compliance with the requirements of the electoral laws.

3. The Political Parties Electoral Referendum Act of 2000 places requirements on all political parties for the establishment of the Treasurer position.

4. The law requires this Treasurer to keep an up-to-date record of all the activities and as such we have the Treasurer as [David Gomadza] and any changes will have to be reported to the Electoral Commission.

5. To make sure that the party complies with the requirements of the law and the Electoral Commission through the PPERA the Treasurer will head a small team to be employed by the party to be responsible for the finances of the party.

6. A financial Committee must be appointed by the Party leader who is also the President.

82. ARTICLE 12

83. THE DISCIPLINARY AND APPEALS PROCESS 84. NATIONAL APPEALS TRIBUNAL.

1. The National Executive Power must appoint members of the National Appeals Tribunals who will sit as judges to hear appeals regarding the

constitution and all other party issues.

2. The National Secretary to organize and appoint or oversee the process in which judges sit to hear the case.

3. Judges for the Appeals Tribunals can be three or more and each has to sit and hear a case.

4. Complicated cases might require all three to sit at once as the judge's panel. 5. Normally their decision is final, but an appeal can be made for the case to be heard by a different judge if there are material things and facts of law issues. 6. They have and can overrule the decision of the lower branch or committee. 7. They can substitute the decision with theirs.

8. They can send the case back to be reconsidered.

9. Must consider all cases regarding the constitution and compliance with all rights and obligations of members.

10. To appoint or remove any judge of the National Appeal Tribunal all

The National Executive members must vote, and a two-thirds majority is enough to appoint or remove that judge.

11. The National Appeal Tribunal only hears the appeal after all processes have been exhausted and within time periods, but the party leader can waive the time limits if the issues are material and

fundamental to the law or critical to the party's principles.

12. Appeals can be applied for within four weeks of the decision of the lower branch in writing to the Appeals Tribunal.

13. Who must arrange a hearing assuming all channels have been exhausted within two weeks of receiving the appeal?

14. Must consider all procedural aspects to determine if they can hear a case but the party leader can waiver such a requirement.

15. Must put in writing all their decisions information about the appellant and the National Executive Power.

16. Their decision is binding and becomes case law.

17. A library must be established to make this case law available to all.

18. The National Executive must review all recommendations and implement these to be proactive.

19. They must recommend if amendments to the constitution are needed. 20. The tribunal designs and implements a code of conduct in carrying out the appeals.

85. THE DISCIPLINARY PROCESS
1. The code of conduct to be written in the bylaws of all-party branches.

2. The party leader, the Secretary, and the National Executive Power to write down the bylaws using this constitution as the guiding principles.

3. All complaints to be submitted in writing to the Secretary are appointed by the leader. Complaints to be heard in less than a week.

4. The Disciplinary Committee decides in writing; to inform the person of his rights and the rights of appeal if any. Stating the time limits and who and where to send the appeal.

5. A clear process that must be followed.

6. The party leader has the right to waive time limits if the case is material and an error of the law.

86. THE DISCIPLINARY COMMITTEE

1. Failure to comply with the requirements of the constitution, by-laws, and regulations will result in penalties or the need for a disciplinary meeting. The party leader must ensure that a party disciplinary committee exists to hear cases where members have disobeyed the rules.

a. Every member and employee on joining shall declare in writing.

when joining or signing employment documents that he or she will

not.

2. Be involved in acts that conflict with the values and rules of the party. 3. That he or she will not be in competition with the party.

4. That the member should not join another political party whose views conflict with the party's views.

5. But when a breach occurs the issue must be sent to the disciplinary committee who will hear the case and pass judgment.

6. The member in breach must be informed that he can appeal and attend a meeting where he can bring a friend or be represented by appointed members of the party who will act in his or her best interest.

7. Time frames; two weeks to make an appeal and four weeks to appeal to the party leader or National Executive Power.

8. If still not resolved and issues are material, the party leader can forward this to the global leader for the final say.

9. Usually, the Party leader's decision is final.

87. ARTICLE 13

88. RULES ON MEETINGS AND PROCEDURES.

1. The quorum is seven for the meeting to go ahead.

2. For the meeting to convene, there must be at least three-party officials or more if the other party officer holds one or more positions e.g., the leader who also happens to be the treasurer. In most cases, there must be a party leader and or the appointed Chairperson or deputy specifically appointed for

meetings, the Treasurer, and the Secretary at any given meeting.

3. Meetings to be held once every month unless it is a campaigning period which can determine the frequency. These should be on the last weekend of the month.

4. The Annual General Meeting is to be held once every year after August and before 1 December where the progress is discussed for that year. Notice of four weeks to be given to all members, especially those with voting rights.

5. Motions to be discussed at the meeting to be handed to the person responsible, especially the Chairperson or Secretary, two weeks before the date of the meeting.

6. Where there is voting; to appoint new members to different positions for the new year.

7. Time to set new agendas and challenges.

8. A chance for the party leader to pitch the members and ask questions, suggestions, etc.

9. Time for the Treasurer to give an update on the financial situation of the party.

10. A time to provide and collect information to be used for the compilation of the financial statements of the party.

11. Voting can be by raising hands or electronically and where there is a tie the party leader or chairperson can make the final vote; the decider.

12. The meeting shall be recorded as minutes. These minutes must state the date, time and venue of the meeting including the start time of the meeting.

13. The minutes must indicate those who were present at the meeting stating the full name and the role of the person.

14. It must state who was absent and why.

15. The minutes must record in note point the matters arising from the meeting and what happened, and issues raised.

16. The minutes must also include the next date and time of the meeting as agreed in the meeting.

89. ARTICLE 14

90. THE KEEPING UP OF THE PARTY'S ACCOUNTS

1. Detailed listings of all the roles, identifying and allocating tasks to the people and putting in place a process that makes it mandatory to comply with the law.

requirements.

2. There must be a system in place that is checked and followed and proven that it makes the party comply with all the requirements.

3. A compliance officer role to oversee this must be appointed and or the party leader to take the leading role to make sure this is so.

4. There must be testing of the procedures, way before the deadline.

5. Document and standardization to be adopted with the party leader or chairperson or secretary be chosen as the authorizing authority signing off documents after the check listing and auditing to all in line with the constitution and the requirements of other laws like the PPERA.

6. The paperwork and documentation must be kept, and copies kept at a different location in electronic form advisably given to the party's agent to keep.

7. A clear workflow plan to be drawn up to show who specifically is responsible for the finance, the running of day-to-day, dealing with all queries, external forces, and other organizations with them. same objectives and values as those of our party

8. The name of the authorizing authority who signs off everything must be written down on the workflow chart and there must be easy access to this information. 9. Make sure you appoint a Party Agent.

10. This person can be politically neutral, usually external, who has the mandate to lodge disclosure with the relevant body.

11. This person must also keep records of the party at their office, which is not the same as the party's headquarters.

91. RULES FOR FORMING TOMORROW'S WORLD ORDER'S COMMITTEES.

1. The following guidelines and bylaws must be used to form any party committees.

2. The Ultimate Executive Power and or the Ultimate Party leader to form all global committees e.g., the Financial Committee, the Judiciary Committee, The Enforcing Committee, The Standing Committee, etc. At the national level the National Executive Power and or the National Party Leader to appoint the committee leader who will appoint and allocate tasks, etc.

3. All committees where the country-specific laws stipulate that registration is required and must be registered; to do so and the link to the party be declared that the committee will be responsible for the day-to-day running of

Tomorrow's World Order.

4. The committee must field a candidate to enter the contest with the hope of representing the party at the national committee level.

5. Appointed committee leader to put a committee hierarchy and task structure clearly defining who is who and what they do in the committee.

6. Must have all processes that ensure day-to-day operations and compliance is met.

7. A compliance officer can be appointed to check compliance with the constitution and all country-specific laws.

8. All committees to be guided and must abide by the party's laws, constitution and bylaws and must acknowledge that they exist only to fulfill the tasks of Tomorrow's World Order.

9. They must not compete, frustrate, or bring into disreputation the values of Tomorrow's World Order.

10. Must acknowledge that they are quasi-subsidiaries of Tomorrow's World Order.

11. Committees must be involved in ongoing activities e.g., promoting the party through campaigns and fundraising.

12. Must publish and advertise party materials; printing leaflets and newsletters, etc. and remaining active.

13. All national committees have their own headquarters that can be or separate from party headquarters, etc.

14. Must hold the Committee convention for the party's work, etc.

15. The National Executive Power of each country to create bylaws to govern the functions of all committees in line with the constitution or country rules. 16. Where permanent committees don't exist, there can be temporary committees during presidential or prime-ministerial election years that can help with the campaigning and all day-to-day operations of the campaigning year.

92. NAMES OF COMMITTEES AND THE DUTIES OF EACH COMMITTEE.
1. Every committee must have a chair, a secretary, treasurer, press officer, and a membership secretary.

2. All national committees to hold annual general meetings were new

committee members can be selected, appointed, or voted for to their respective tasks.

3. Committee to abide by all files and reports reporting requirements within the constitution, bylaws, and national rules, etc.

4. New committee members are to be elected or appointed every

year at the annual general meeting or the national conference.

5. To be nominated on merit by the committee leaders and some might be politically neutral in that they are needed because of their qualifications

rather than affiliation to our political party but better if they don't belong to a party that has views, we are against.

93. FINANCIAL COMMITTEE.
1. The Party Leader; the President, has powers to appoint a Financial

Committee and has the mandate to do so in order for the party to comply with the requirements of the PPERA and other political parties' laws.

2. The Party Leader must appoint, name, and record the members of the team and what their objectives are and what is required of them.

3. There must be a plan showing who is who as members. What duties each is responsible for doing? When and how often they are to do what they are supposed to do.

4. The Financial Committee must formulate, devise, implement, monitor, and plan the internal financial controls to be used and be adopted by the

committee and party in order to meet the requirements of the PPERA.

5. The financial Committee must create systems that will make sure that the party adheres to the requirements of PPERA.

6. The committee must observe and use the following procedures.

94. FINANCE.

1. All donations, contributions, raised money, loans, etc. are to be used in accordance with the constitution and for the realization of the party's

objectives.

2. Any payments must be made by the Treasurer and depending on the amount involved might require the signature of the party leader or Secretary.

3. Procedures must be in place to comply with the compliance rules, which means all accounts to be audited and assessed once a year before the treasurer sends them to the Electoral Commission.

4. Expenses can be paid to the Executive Powers for expenses incurred during performing their duties.

95. ESTABLISH THE NATIONAL POLICY COMMITTEE

1. The size of the party determines if a separate National Policy Committee is required or not.

2. Must meet the requirements of the procedural aspect of the party following the guidelines in this constitution.

3. A certain proportion shall be women and members of ethnic background and or youth representatives.

4. Shall meet often especially in campaigning years at least every two months. 5. Shall research, assess, decide, and recommend issues that can end up as policy topics that year.

6. Shall debate and advise the National Executive Power and the Party leader on hot topics that need urgent priority etc.

7. Members shall be elected according to expertise in certain areas

but must be voluntary but a fund to be set aside for publication and producing of

documents to be forwarded to the National Executive Power.

8. Usually, for members but open to everyone, the only requirement is to advise of intention to attend two weeks before the meeting for seating

arrangements to be made.

9. They must then select delegates to address the National Executive

Committee at least once a year at a special conference where policy

formulation will take place deciding which areas to focus on the next following year.

96. FORMING A NATIONAL ADVOCATE COMMITTEE.
1. Must be recruited by the party leader as they reflect or must mirror the party leader.

2. It might be answerable to the Chairperson who is appointed by the party leader and often covers for the party leader.

3. A team of highly motivated members must be assembled to act as the party's advocates.

4. This will be their sole role as a new party with a completely new out of the norm strategy. We need a strong advocate team to sell our idea to everyone. At the start of the campaign, odds might be against us as people can't change the tried and trusted.

5. But a team that knows our strength can effectively sell our ideas. The party leader and the National Executive Power must assess and choose from volunteers and assemble a team.

6. But the leader of the advocate team can be appointed and can be paid to act for a limited period in that capacity to train a voluntary leader among members. 7. After a certain time, his or her role can be terminated by giving two weeks' notice before replacing him or her.

8. The new leader should take over and spearhead the advocacy. Members shall operate on a daily basis traveling around the country to shopping centers etc. with approval of the local authorities pitching people.

9. Must be trained; free training, voluntary with expenses like traveling and food covered by the party. The treasurer or Secretary to arrange such a setting. Code of conduct to be adhered to.

10. There must be a qualifying period before the roles are paid. Three months continuous can have one recruited to the permanent paid role. All members at one point once a month must meet and spend time with the party leader.

11. Must reflect the leader and in the future; quick advancement to be able to apply for party leaders or youth leader's roles.

12. Apart from advocating must advise everyone of their rights.

13. To vote in all elections and referendums.

14. Must inform every one of their rights and obligations to join and get involved in all party activities.

15. That they can and must join and put their names forward to be elected to different party positions.

97. ARTICLE 15

98. TOMORROW'S WORLD ORDER'S FINANCIAL PLAN

99. GLOBAL RESERVE BANK.

1. This will act as the world's reserve bank accepting deposits of all new fresh printed money of each and every country.

2. Managing funds and reserves keeping an up-to-date account of all

transactions.

3. Managing our own currency, the FutureGoldCoin making sure that the digital currency is run and well managed to check its security and suitability of use both as a world currency for all transactions and as a reserve

currency.

4. Involved in the issuing of our FutureGoldCoin to all nations in proportion to the deposited funds.

5. Assessing the circulating levels making sure that every country has enough of our money.

6. Maintaining savings accounts of all nations; calculating interest earned. 7. The global reserve bank leader who is appointed by the Ultimate Executive Power to manage the deposited funds and invest some to generate more. 8. To set aside a percentage of the reserves towards global development projects liaising with the Project Development Team.

9. The reserve development fund will allocate funds for projects to be

completed in weeks or months by ensuring that money for the

whole project is available even before the projects start.

10. The idea is to carry out huge projects before even being paid a penny or a cent of the money.

11. We shall use the deposits as collateral and as long as the nation is sovereign, we shall use this as the easy ability to print money and their word as a guarantee that we will get the money back.

This speeds up the building and completion of projects even without receiving any money.

12. To make sure that all nations deposit a base value of the deposits; that is the minimum reserve that forms the minimum balance.

13. To report to the National Executive Powers and maybe twice a year all to meet to discuss progress and plans for the future.

14. Twice as a minimum a year to link with the Ultimate Executive Power to update on progress and plan for the future.

15. To make sure that all nations are using two currencies; their sovereign currency and our digital currency by auditing countries reporting those who are not to the enforcement power to be appointed initially by the Ultimate Executive Power or Ultimate Global Leader.

16. To form multinational companies.

17. To arrange the funding in advance of all that is needed.

18. To offer loans to multinationals to carry out swift projects.

19. To assess the savings of all nations and using this as collateral to provide infrastructure and services needed by that country and start the building of projects even without payment as long as approved by the Ultimate Executive Power and or the Global Party

Leader.

20. To determine the times for the global printing of new money.

21. To put corrective fiscal measures to flatten out any obstacles, etc.

22. To report to the Ultimate Executive Power and the Global President or Party Leader.

100. TOMORROW'S WORLD ORDER LTD REG 12326946
1. Already registered on 21 November 2019 in the United Kingdom under the Companies Act 2006 as a private company limited by shares. Code: Activities of political organizations.

2. Normally to be registered by the Ultimate Executive Power and or by the Global Party Leader.

3. Its main reason for its establishment is to source funds through investment as well as donations and sponsorship.

4. To act as a perpetual fund that will fund our party through the proceeds of the investment so that every nation can receive a grant donated from this fund to help establish T.W.O party all over the globe providing easily available funds for political agendas.

5. Must appoint a dedicated team of fundraisers who can fund the party. 6. Financial Director to coordinate fundraising from individuals and

corporations.

7. Together with the Secretary, the committee and the National Executive come up with a code of conduct for fundraising that maintains the party's credibility ensuring that rules are followed, and people don't do anything that will make people not trust the party.

8. Violations to be dealt with within the disciplinary process.

9. The Fundraising Director must accept any funding towards the party.

101. ASSOCIATION FOR THE FOUNDING MEMBERS.

1. The founding members can use the rules of this constitution to the group and form an association.

2. They must select a chairperson.

3. Can contribute to the association.

4. The purpose is to bring great ideas together and to continue pursuing the values and growth of the party bringing all great minds together.

5. Patrons who are lifelong donors can join the association.

6. The members become delegates for the National Conference.

7. The association can nominate members to represent them at all levels from the national committee to the Ultimate Executive Power.

8. Normally once every three years can nominate members to attend the Ultimate Executive Power meetings abroad.

9. Can nominate members for the top job. Global leadership.

10. Automatically qualify to apply for the global leadership role.

102. FUNDRAISING AND MONEY DONATED TO THE PARTY.

1. The funds from investment in Tomorrow's World Order Ltd is used to fund the party; the profits made can be transferred to

Tomorrow's World Order's party accounts, money that can be used for paying employees, for consumables and services, etc.

2. The donated money to be invested in the company and the proceeds only to be channeled to Tomorrow's World Order party account.

3. Tomorrow's World Order LTD to be registered in each country. A dedicated team to be established to source funds from potential donors for the party money that can be used to provide capital for Tomorrow's World Order LTD money that it can invest as a company to further fund the political party.

4. A huge recruitment drive of fundraisers to fund our party.

103. FUTUREGOLDCOIN DEVELOPMENT EXECUTIVE.
1. The Ultimate Executive Power and or the Global Party Leader will appoint the FutureGoldCoin Development Executive to.

2. design its own digital currency,

3. develop,

4. implement,

5. monitor,

6. check and

7. audit for security and feasibility, etc. continuously.

8. This executive is to be involved in the implementation of our digital currency globally and its maintenance.

9. To establish Executive branches globally.

10. To recruit a team of experts who see the implementation and monitoring in every country solving issues that might arise.

11. Monthly official meetings and quarterly of all global teams and at least two annual conferences together with the Ultimate Executive Power.

104. UNIVERSAL ENFORCING AND JUDICIARY EXECUTIVE POWER.

1. The Ultimate Executive Power and or the Global Party Leader to establish the Universal Enforcing and Judiciary Executive Power which has a duty to enforce our laws globally.

2. This executive power will further establish executive powers in every county that will enforce our laws.

3. Our laws are universal, and crime is punishable in any other country irrespective of where it was committed.

4. To appoint and train a special enforcement unit that is directly answerable to the Ultimate Executive Power and or the Global Leader showing their powers to remove anyone's individual immunity.

5. Must bring people to justice no matter where the crimes were committed.

6. The Ultimate Executive Power and or the Global Party Leader to appoint a new judiciary system to deal with violators.

7. These to enforce our laws and rules globally safeguarding our interests and everyone's interests globally.

105. ARTICLE 16

106. MECHANISMS FOR CHANGING THE CONSTITUTION

1. This constitution provides the guiding line for changing and

amending the constitution. 2. The party's decision-making board can give notice in writing to all voters and members with rights giving notice of two to four weeks.

3. Must arrange the venue and time and be involved in the voting and as a general rule two-thirds is enough to amend the constitution.

4. Material changes must be referred to as the global Ultimate Executive Power and the Global Party Leader who will authorize the go-ahead of the amendments.

5. The quorum at such meetings must be greater or equal to seven with each member having a single vote apart from the party leader who can cast another vote in case of a tie.

107. RULES ON AMENDMENTS TO THE CONSTITUTION.
1. Intentions to amend the constitution should be announced to everyone four weeks before the Annual General Meeting or a special Extraordinary General Meeting is held at any time as long as the members are notified of the

intention two weeks before the date of the EGM.

2. This is normally for minor amendments but if the changes are substantial, the global branch must be notified, and all proposals are forwarded to this global branch who will look at the proposed changes in order to check if the changes are material to require the signature of the authorizing authority.

3. After authorization the T.W.O [UK] branch can now announce the intention to make amendments two weeks before the day of the meeting.

4. Everyone with voting rights must attend and vote.

5. Two-thirds of the votes are enough for the constitution to be

amended. 6. Any changes to be forwarded to the global branch to be synchronized if needed globally.

108. ARTICLE 17

109.ESTABLISHMENT OF STATE AND TERRITORY BRANCHES

1. Apart from this, the constitution also follows local country-specific laws in branch and territory establishment and also the party leaders to check with the global leader to make sure that the national goals are in line with the global goals.

2. The party leader together with the National Executive Power can establish or nominate someone to be responsible for the expansion.

3. To check and create bylaws as seen fit.

4. Representation can be addressed by local bylaws and the party leader together with the National Executive Power to oversee or delegate such tasks.

5. To draw up a detailed expansion plan showing dates and time frames needed to establish a branch in other territory and to complement the national and global plan.

6. To set up a team with a project manager or leader to arrange the funding and liaise with the national party leader to appoint roles to fill these new branches.

110. ENDORSING CANDIDATES.

1. The Party Leaders together with the National Executive Power to put together a detailed plan of endorsing candidates who stand in all elections as this is the main objective of the party.

2. The candidates must understand and have the aim to contest, win and take office so that our party can realize and implement its

goals.

3. The party Secretary or Chairperson or any office role deemed to be so on request by the Party Leader must organize a public meeting or gathering like a conference four weeks before the date and announce inviting people to

attend.

4. Endorse only candidates that have signed and agreed to comply with our constitution and standards for credibility purposes.

5. Must work together with the Campaigning Committee to rally support and ensure full capacity or a large gathering.

6. Distribution of campaigning materials well ahead of the date to ensure a large turnout.

7. The Party Leader to endorse the candidate to run for elections.

8. Meetings to be held during the week at night after work or weekends where the party leader must travel to the constituent.

9. At the conference the candidate to take the stage together with the Party Leader who endorses him or her publicly and live on party broadcast.

Heralding to the world that he or she is the candidate to represent.

Tomorrow's World Order in the upcoming election.

10. The Party Leader publicly endorsed the candidate giving him 100% support before rallying everyone to back the candidate.

11. Leaflets and other publications to be distributed before and after the

endorsement with the picture of the candidate visible for all to see.

12. All endorsements must be viewed and regarded as Official Endorsement with a procedure in place to write and record down this in party books and documents showing the date, time, venue and who endorsed the person and a picture of the party leader with the candidate taken and put in a file.

13. Only party leaders have powers to endorse and in case of absences the conference can be postponed or a party leader from another country be

invited to perform the ceremony.

14. Anyone from the Ultimate global Executive Power has the right to endorse and can do so as authorized by the Global Party Leader.

15. Ideally, the endorsement to be broadcast on national television and the Secretary or Treasurer arranges that or delegate such activities.

111. ARTICLE 18

112. COMMENCEMENT

1. The party leaders and the National Executive Power Board to choose a date, a venue and send out notices giving four weeks' notice to all who can vote to invite them to attend and vote so that the constitution is commenced, and this is noted as the day the constitution takes effect.

2. All participants to vote to adopt the constitution signing to confirm that.

3. The party leader and the National Executive Power to sign the adoption motion.

4. A date is to be set aside and announced to all informing the willingness to vote in order to commence the constitution on that

specific date.

5. Notice to be sent four weeks given as notice to all those with voting rights and two weeks' notice to members to attend.

6. The National Executive and the Party leader and every member must be present to cast a vote in favor of commencement.

7. Everyone on the day to vote to adopt the constitution on that specific date and time.

8. The National Executive Power and the Party Leader to sign the motion of commencing the constitution.

9. All this to be publicized in the Official Magazine of the party and most local newspapers.

10. An Official Magazine to be printed and distributed free showing the day the constitution commenced.

11. This date to be noted and written down in all official documents and be regarded as the commencement date of the constitution and thereafter

everyone to be abided by it.

113. ARTICLE 19

114. COALITION, MERGERS, AND DISSOLUTION

1. Dissolving the party in a specific area or branch requires first the approval of the Global Party Leader and that of the Ultimate Executive Power.

2. A letter of intent must be sent to the Global Headquarters four weeks before the intended meeting to vote to dissolve the branch or party.

3. Members and or assets can be passed onto another branch or

party where necessary. 4. After the voting to dissolve the Party Leader or representative of the branch must inform the Global Leader no later than two weeks after the meeting to seek the

authorizing signatures to dissolve that branch or party.

5. The Global Leader's decision is final.

6. Where a coalition is the only option the party shall enter into a coalition with other parties but for a defined time e.g., a term before another general election.

7. Our stance and values shall not change but we shall facilitate the coalition for the agreed time.

8. The National Conference can lay down the terms of the coalition and make sure that this goes smoothly.

9. Mergers are between the same parties and are okay, but such arrangements must be approved by the Conference and the Ultimate Executive Power and the Global

President.

10. Any winding up of the party is to be authorized by the Global Party Leader or the Ultimate Executive Power in case of his or her absence who has the final word and no subsidiary party groups can wound up the party until after

authorization in which a meeting must take place and the members with voting rights vote. Two-thirds of the votes are enough for the dissolution to take place.

115. INTERPRETATION

In this constitution the following words are defined here.

1. T.W.O means Tomorrow's World Order

2. AGM means Annual General Meeting

3. NEP means National Executive Power

4. NEPB means National Executive Power Board

5. PPERA means Political Parties, Elections and Referendum Act 2000

6. UEP means Ultimate Executive Power

7. NSRGC means New Single Reserve Global Currency

8. FCI stands for FutureGoldCoin our digital currency

9. GRB means Global Reserve Bank, our reserves bank.

Visit www.twofuture.world

info@twofuture.world

00447719210295

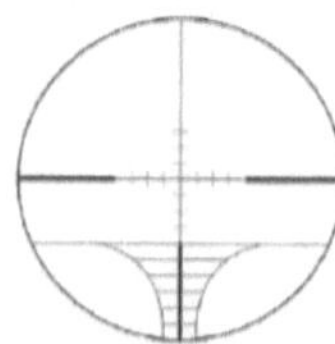
TOMORROW'S WORLD ORDER
STOP!
KILLING WOMEN
AND CHILDREN.
www.twofuture.world
Tomorrow's
World
Order
A New Law & Order. Dealing with
Threats of Invasions, Wars and War
Crimes
David Gomadza

ABOUT DAVID GHOMADZA

I am the founder of Tomorrow's World Order.
The First Global President of The World.
00447719210295
Info@twofuture.world
www.twofuture.world

The Constitution: Tomorrow's World Order.